I developed this one three minutes longer and got it a good week.

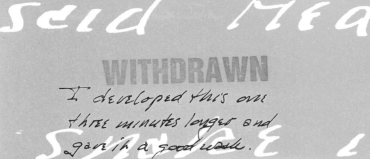

Rauni, the Txuk chieftain, on his way to new village. That's his gun I'm carrying; I don't own one.

So strange and wonderful. This enchanted land is casting a spell over me from which I shall never escape.

The Machiguenges live on the jungled mountainside; tough to land a plane here!

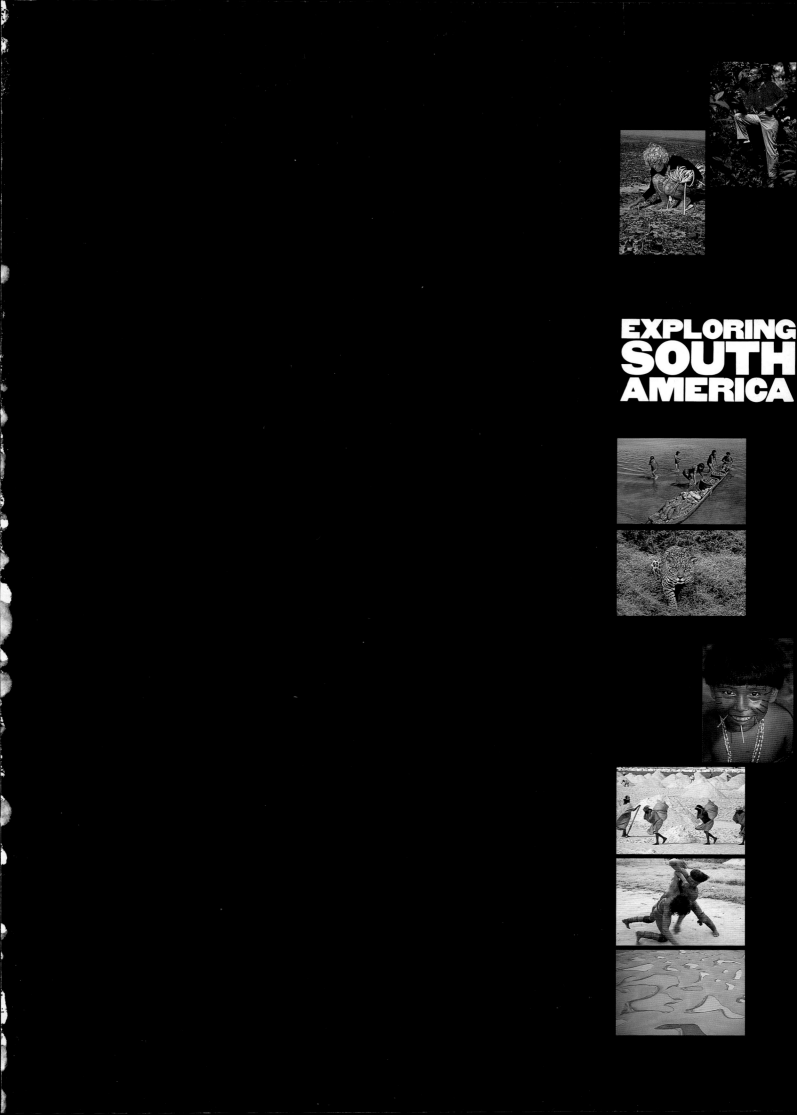

EXPLORING SOUTH AMERICA

ORING

JTH

McIntyre

RICA

Design by

Drenttel Doyle Partners

Clarkson N. Potter, Inc, Publishers

New York

Copyright © 1990 by Loren McIntyre
Photographs on pages 1, second from
bottom; 8; 28; 30, left; 93; 107; 111, top;
156, third from left; and 191, bottom
Loren McIntyre © National Geographic
Society

Published by Clarkson N. Potter, Inc.,
201 East 50th Street,
New York, New York 10022, and
distributed by Crown Publishers, Inc.

CLARKSON N. POTTER, POTTER,
and colophon are trademarks
of Clarkson N. Potter, Inc.

Manufactured in Japan

Library of Congress Cataloging-
in-Publication Data

McIntyre, Loren, 1917–
    Exploring South America / by Loren
McIntyre.—1st ed.
        p.   cm.
    Includes index.
    1. South America—Description and
    travel— – Views.
    I. Title.
F2225.M37   1989
918—dc20   89-3966
                                              CIP
ISBN 0-517-56134-4

10 9 8 7 6 5 4 3 2 1

First Edition

To Sue

CONTENTS

Under the equatorial sun the steel deck of the 10,000-ton SS *West Notus* scorches my bare feet. I take the helm. A Brazilian river pilot sings out our course into the Pará estuary, one of the mouths of the Amazon.

Opposite, Death in the Rain Forest.

Brazil, 6° 13′ south latitude, 56° 10′

west longitude. 2 October 1976.

As in tapestries adorning castle walls in Portugal, the river is embroidered with boats carrying lateen sails, dark red, bright blue. They resemble the transoceanic caravels that first explored these waterways.

    West Notus skirts a jungle shore and anchors off the town of Belém to load Brazil nuts and mahogany. We swing six hours to and six hours fro in the world's highest freshwater tides. Despite the heat I must dress in coat and tie to go ashore. Men have to wear jackets even to board a trolley car in tropical Brazil. Women of Belém, more thinly clad, powder their throats with talc scented with crushed blossoms of aromatic trees, such as those along Avenida da República.

    A sudden downpour drives me into a *cine* featuring a "talking picture," *Caravan*. The plush theater seat is as hot as the cushions of the gypsy wagon where Charles Boyer bundles with Loretta Young. Afterward, from my balcony in the Café e Hotel da Paz, I listen to passersby singing a hit from the movie "The Wine Song." My room, with furniture of inlaid Brazilian hardwoods, costs forty cents, nearly half my daily wage.

    Next day I go to a waterfront market named Ver-o-Peso ("Watch the Weight"!). I press through displays of parrots and pelts, of perfumes and packets of mysterious charms, including private parts of dolphins, of captive ocelots, snakes in baskets, and murky iced drinks. The sweating crowds of townsfolk and rivermen are of Portuguese, African, American Indian, and mixed descent. *West Notus*'s doctor and I heft a fifteen-foot boa constrictor, too heavy to carry on board. We settle for some big snakeskins and little live reptiles to take to California.

    West Notus sails for Barbados on a glassy sea. Jocko, a woolly monkey, swings from the rigging by his tail. George the Oiler's two marmosets hug each other desperately. Louie the Cook bought a cage of *gralhas* bright of feather and gruff of voice. A three-toed sloth hangs above the bunk where Jerry the Cadet lazes twelve hours of every twenty-four. . . .

    This account is based on a letter mailed from Barbados to my family in Seattle, 15 September 1935. The letter ends, "This enchanted land is casting a spell over me, from which I shall never escape." Although the ingenuous statement, like the writer, was fresh out of high school, it was prophetic, for that voyage shaped the rest of my life.

    The word *Amazon* had made free with my daydreams even before I grew up. In 1926, Seattle newspapers reported that British Colonel Percy H. Fawcett, a famous frontiersman and fellow of the Royal Geographical Society, had

disappeared in the jungle. Fawcett was a mystic given to such fantasies as sighting sixty-foot snakes that wailed. He had been searching for the capital of some Atlantis race he had read about in a faded parchment. At age nine I had not yet learned to doubt the daily news, so I believed that Mrs. Fawcett was receiving in England telepathic messages from her lost husband in Brazil. He was rumored to have become a white god of the Xingú River, the Amazon's most mysterious tributary.

One night in 1928 my crystal set crackled with a radio report from another noted explorer, Commander George M. Dyott, Royal Navy, who was searching the Xingú for traces of Fawcett. I never imagined that in thirty years I would be South American production manager of a Hollywood film based on the Fawcett and Dyott expeditions—and a decade after that would stumble upon Dyott, at eighty-six a recluse in an equatorial redoubt.

By age twelve I had read everything in my neighborhood library on South America and had tried to write a short story—I have it at hand—that begins, "Pink flashes of gunfire blossomed from the forest along the Amazon's shore." That year I spent six weeks' income from my paper route to buy a Kodak folding camera in a hockshop.

From age seventeen on, sailing the seven seas to five continents in the merchant marine, the only serious gunfire I witnessed was in China during a Japanese attack on Shanghai. I managed to evade the experience of actually facing those "pink flashes" until World War II, when I was gunnery officer of a warship in the Pacific. In that war the enemy sent SS *West Notus*—and eight other ships I had sailed on—to Davy Jones's locker.

Since then I have spent most of my life in South America. Such shooting as I have seen there has been not along the Amazon but around my house and office during insurrections. Sometimes Indians opened up with Mausers when my boat trespassed into their fishing grounds on the Bolivian shore of Lake Titicaca. I go unarmed. Shooting only with a camera, I have taken nearly one million photographs in South America.

I shot them on journeys through the continent in search of images that might excite a sense of wonder. I have not gone looking for thrills or lost cities, although I have found both. Nor have I explored frontiers of knowledge there, as did the naturalist Baron Alexander von Humboldt and hosts of later scientists. My quest (if I dare presume that photo expeditions merit such an elegant noun) has been to record phenomena—not events—that few people would otherwise get to see, such as hidden waterfalls and exotic creatures. I gather pictures of things apt to disappear forever: a giant otter, a rain-forest Indian making bark clothing. I do not subscribe to any photographic mystique and have no theories to expound. I am not trying, as some young photographers put it, to "find myself." I am not lost— though one of my Indian friends thinks so.

"Loren, your pictures lie," declares Oswaldo Guayasamín, an internationally famous Indian artist of Quito, Ecuador, and friend of Fidel Castro. "You prettify the ugly truths of this cruel continent while my people weep."

"Oswaldo, your paintings distort the truth. You deny that peasants smile." I contend that, with so many reporters bent on tallying misery, I am content to capture a bit of the beauty that abounds.

I shoot as many as 10,000 pictures to achieve the three dozen images that editors may select to portray a South American country for readers of my

National Geographic magazine articles. Since it is impossible to illustrate an entire nation even with unlimited pages, the few published images had better be memorable.

While shooting country stories I am never sure what to look for. On the road I sometimes feel dislocated in time and space from the opportunity for a big picture. I speed past a thatched hut at the edge of a forest, beguiled by a glimpse of a girl poised at her window, hands crossed on the sill. The scene fades behind me and the second thoughts begin. Had I indeed seen a Gioconda smile and eyes like emeralds set in cinnamon? If I had caught it on film, might her portrait hang one day in the wardroom of some future spaceship? Why hurry on, why not stop? Regret grows stronger and finally wrenches me around. I hurry back several miles. But, as in a nightmare, darkness falls before I get there; she is nowhere to be seen.

The perfect picture—if there is such a thing—forever eludes me for shortage of time, for lack of luck, or for poverty of artistic vision. Or maybe even for failure to seek divine grace, as was required of the knights errant of Arthurian legend. Wandering the wilderness in search of the ultimate photograph can be as unfulfilling as their quest for the Holy Grail.

o v e r l e a f
A desiccated scorpion suspended among elixirs and magic charms displayed in the Banca Chama (Lure Shop) attracts a Far Eastern tourist at Ver-O-Peso market on Belém's waterfront in Brazil.

Once, without realizing it, I captured an almost flawless image. I was kneeling at the open door of a little airplane, camera at my eye, winging low over a sea of green—the Amazon forest of Brazil. A pattern in white flashed before my lens and I snapped it. So swiftly was it gone that I did not remember it afterward.

When it was published as "The Best of the Best" in the book *Photo-journalism/3, 1978*, one editor cited its "elegant composition, in terms of both form and color, and its painterly qualities." Another called it "beautiful, the kind of thing you could live with on the wall for a long, long time. And taken, I might add, from the perfect distance." Those critics may not have realized that I controlled neither composition nor distance. *Death in the Rain Forest*—which opens this prologue— is just a snapshot.

Its casual origin reminds me of the achievements of Martín Chambi, an Indian who owned a photo shop and portrait studio in the ancient Inca capital of Cuzco, Peru. I met Chambi there in 1948, before tourists began to come by the thousands to visit nearby Machu Picchu, the lost city of the Incas, that most awesome spectacle in all South America. Sometimes business was so slack that Chambi did little but lean on the counter in his shop, point to his pictures on the walls, and argue the merits of Marxism with "Yankee imperialists" such as I. More in the interest of filling the till than in some higher calling, Chambi would shoulder his tripod when times got tight and tour the surrounding highlands taking pictures of rural families and festivals. I do not think he was self-consciously recording for posterity the faces and costumes of his people, but in the end he did just that.

After his death, a cult grew up around memories of Martín Chambi, with photo archivists lauding his dedication to a presumable cause—be it ethnic, social, or historical. My view of Chambi's cause is that he simply wanted to take pictures that people admired—and of course get paid for them.

Like Chambi, or a glassblower at a county fair for that matter, I am delighted to have you looking over my shoulder.

A R L I N G T O N ,   V I R G I N I A
2 4   M A R C H   1 9 8 9

"Big roar" at the mouth of the A M A Z O N ... an exchange of gifts with the W A U R Á chief ... dancing the T A U A R A U A N Ã ... river travel by dugout and luxury liner ... operatic flight with the M A N O F L A M A N C H A ... the impossible dream—panning for gold at C A N T A G A L O ... the R I O N E G R O by floatplane and cabin cruiser ... captured by frontier guards on the O R I N O C O ... discovery of the source and the naming of L A G U N A M C I N T Y R E

THE AMAZON

Splitting into labyrinthine waterways, *opposite,* the Amazon carries runoff from one-third of the South American continent down to the sea. Few humans dwell in its 200-mile-wide delta, saturated by cloudbursts almost every afternoon.

Come hell or high water I was determined to photograph the legendary *pororoca*—"the big roar"—an oceanic tidal wave said to periodically overpower the Amazon River at its mouth. I had never seen the wave and had never met anyone who could tell me where to find it.

    The *pororoca* was first reported by the discoverer of the Amazon, Vincente Yáñez Pinzón, who had been skipper of Columbus's *Niña*. Pinzón was leading his own expedition across the equator in 1500 when the ocean became muddy. Water drawn from the sea tasted fresh. Then a towering wave swept Pinzón's caravel shoreward and into the wide mouth of a river. The Spaniards cried out to the Virgin; the wave subsided. Pinzón gave thanks to Santa María de la Mar Dulce, Saint Mary of the Sweetwater Sea, which became the river's first name to appear on maps.

    Years ago the founder of *National Geographic* magazine, Gardiner Hubbard, wrote: "Up from the ocean into this valley an immense tidal wave rolls . . . twice a day, forcing back the current of the Amazon 500 miles and inundating a portion of the flood-plain." Hubbard was mistaken. The wave would have to flow an astonishing eighty miles an hour upstream, then ebb just as fast in order to repeat the tidal cycle twice a day. Encyclopedias in several languages still carry descriptions as fanciful as Hubbard's, while all sorts of vessels from canoes to ocean liners ply the Amazon mainstream untroubled by such a calamity.

    Might a bore occur in a lesser channel? In 1969, I had an opportunity to find out when editors of the *Geographic* asked me to help illustrate the book *Exploring the Amazon* (1970).

    The river is so wide—200 miles when it reaches the ocean—that only astronauts are able to see across the mouth. And only on their way to the moon do they pull away enough to observe the Amazon's entire 4,000-mile length from source to sea. *O Rio Mar,* the Portuguese explorers called it: The River Sea.

    I prowled around the river's mouth in a small seaplane, asking villagers where the bore might be. Eventually I learned from an old fisherman that sixty-mile-wide Caviana Island had been cut in two in 1850 by a devastating *pororoca*. The wave created the Furo de Guajurú, now one of the Amazon's outlets. The fisherman explained that tidal bores appear only in shallow water and that the Furo is mostly less than four fathoms deep. "But the *pororoca* forms only when the full moon is setting and the tide is unusually high," he added.

He once took a city friend fishing at dawn and anchored in the path of the *pororoca*. "When the wave rushed toward us, my friend was terrified. I just sat and fished. The wave suddenly disappeared under us while passing high on both sides. I knew it would. I had deliberately anchored in a deep spot."

As with ocean waves that curl and break when they reach the shallows of a beach, the formation of the *pororoca* depends upon a "bottom effect" that may explain Pinzón's salvation. Apparently the *pororoca* caught his caravel in shallow water and swept it into deeper water, where the wave subsided.

To explore Caviana, I persuaded a Brazilian bush pilot in the port city of Belém to take off at night—illegally—while the full moon was still high in the west. We flew 200 miles northwest across the equator in high, cool air. Daybreak reddened sea and sky and even the jungle mists below. We reached the Furo de Guajurú, the waterway that bisects Caviana, just as the *pororoca* was forming.

A single tall wave curved across the channel. We flew back and forth across the thundering twelve-foot wall of water while it swept upstream, uprooting trees from both banks and rebounding in a splendid succession of resonant waves. I shot roll after roll of film, driven by the certainty that this was the first time the "Big Roar" had ever been photographed from the air. As the moon set, the wave gradually subsided.

We saw no boats, no huts, no signs of human life. Only the pilot and I watched that convulsive struggle of the river with the ocean—or, in truth, of part of the Amazon reversing itself at the moon's command, for all that water at the mouth is fresh. Too often in my South American journeys I have been the sole witness to such wonders, glad that 35mm cameras and film came of age when I did, so that I might share my experiences with others.

By the mid-1970s I had seen all the major Amazon tributaries. They rise in Brazil and five neighboring countries to merge into the greatest moving mass of fresh water on earth. Eight tributaries roughly match in volume, one for one, the world's next largest rivers after the Amazon: Congo (Zaire), Yangtze, Brahmaputra, Ganges, Mississippi, Yenisei, Orinoco, and Lena, in that order. All eight world rivers combined do not equal the average Amazon discharge of sixty million gallons per second—sixty times greater than the Nile.

Contrary to many accounts, the Amazon's discharge does not gush *far out* into the Atlantic. A three- to four-knot ocean current sweeps northwest along the coast to Devil's Island and beyond. Its dominant chocolaty hue comes from the westernmost tributaries, which bring down sediment scoured by rain, wind, and ice from the Andes Mountains of Colombia, Ecuador, Peru, and Bolivia. From the north come black-water tributaries stained by ooze flushed from murky swamps. Blue-water tributaries out of uplands to the south sparkle over diamond-bearing gravel and widen into vast azure lakes before entering the mainstream.

The accent on the last syllable of the blue-water names—Tefé, Coarí, Tapajós, Xingú—suggests the lilt of tribal tongues spoken by aborigines who dwell along their headwaters. The very sound *Xingú* (pronounced Shin-GOO) stirs my memory of slogging nine hours through a swampy forest in 1972 as naked Waurá tribesmen led me to their village. Protocol required that the chief and I *trocar presentes* —"exchange gifts." I gave fishhooks and a mile of ten-pound nylon line

in return for one of the shallow clay urns the Waurá make as a medium of exchange with other Xingú tribes. They took me into the men's house, played massive magic flutes that women are forbidden to glimpse on pain of gang rape, and passed around a ritual cigar of green tobacco.

The half-moon overhead at night was the size the Amazon Basin would appear if you could see it from that far away. I took care not to stare at it too long lest I be suspected of witchcraft. The moon, in Waurá myth, was born of the same jaguar that mothered the Xingú tribes.

The community house I slept in was shaped like a Quonset about one hundred feet long and thatched all the way to the ground. Children had slung my hammock and built under it a smoky fire to ward off mosquitoes and predawn chill. Past midnight I awakened from a dream about hearing an oboe player lost in the woods and recognized the melancholy call of the sobbing owl that frontiersmen call *mãe da lua*, "mother of the moon."

I breakfasted on fish paste folded in torn pieces of *beijú*, huge pancakes of manioc, the starchy root of the only plant I saw them cultivate. I swam in the Batoví, a Xingú tributary, while children fished with bows and arrows. Under a threatening afternoon sky, burly Waurá warriors dressed me in a skirt of *buriti* palm fibers, tied aromatic leaves to my arms, and painted my body with *urucú* paste, a red vegetable dye. They persuaded me to leap and grimace wildly with them in a ritual dance called Tauarauanã until a thunderstorm ended the fun.

Next day the chief gave me another pot. I did not understand that meant my time was up. Later he gave me two larger ones. Eventually he summoned a bearer to carry my basketful of eleven pots, took my elbow, and pointed to the path out of the village. I hastily handed out harpoon points—good-bye gifts—and followed taciturn guides back out through the swamp. The sky was overcast; I soon lost all sense of direction. Not then, but long afterward, I reflected that the Indians could easily have ditched me in the swamp.

Up the Amazon from the Xingú confluence, the next big blue-water tributary out of the south is the Rio Tapajós. Years ago I sailed a dugout canoe along the forested shore of its terminal lake, a blue lagoon ten miles wide and one hundred miles long. I have cruised into the lake a dozen times to picnic on white-sand beaches with passengers of the elegant Greek transatlantic liner *Stella Solaris;* during the Christmas season I lecture on board about the Amazon. But my most far-reaching Tapajós trips have been by single-engine aircraft, the commonest form of transportation in the Amazon valley—after the canoe.

Flight is the key to hidden *garimpos,* the gold and diamond placer mines of the upper Tapajós jungle. But before they strike it rich enough to hire wings, *garimpeiros*—prospectors or miners—can only reach their claims by slashing through oppressive aisles of trees by day with ticks crawling up their legs, and swinging under leaky roofs of leaves by night with ants crawling down their hammock ropes. Thousands of *garimpeiros,* mainly victims of bullets and malaria, rot in unmarked graves.

Three hundred miners were panning gold at a strike called *Cantagalo* ("Cockcrow") concealed in the hills east of the Tapajós town of Jacareacanga ("Lair of the Crocodile"). I flew in beside an elderly Brazilian aviator, whose snug leather helmet and earflaps, scarf of parachute nylon, and fleece-lined bombardier jacket (in such heat!) gave him the air of a barnstormer fond of flying upside down.

He brought an overload of beer and sides of beef in the backseat, and his lap was full of bank notes for buying gold dust. He skimmed just above the unbroken broccoli of the forest crown, waving an unlit cigar and bursting into operatic song.

When I sighted Cantagalo airstrip, a slim slash in the green with three shacks alongside, I interrupted an aria from *The Man of La Mancha*. "The miners all live there?"

"No. Life is too transient for building houses. Those shacks are a company office, a dance hall, and a whorehouse. The *garimpeiros* live in the forest, in hammocks, under lean-tos, some with women, some without, some sick, most of them poor, some getting rich, all of them dreaming the impossible dream."

We landed.

In the forest I met a miner, Araujo, who once found 230 ounces of gold nuggets in a week. He blew a year's take on cars he could not drive and planes he could not fly. Now waist-deep in muck again, he was panning for gold with two assistants, both lepers.

In the office I watched an accountant stir mercury into a pan of pay dirt to soak the gold dust from the dross, then boil off the mercury with a blowtorch, heedless of the deadly vapor. I bolted.

In the dance hall I shared a sad Saturday of Carnival with *garimpeiros* wealthy enough to afford warm dollar-a-bottle Coke and beer and forlorn dollar-a-dance girls. At the whorehouse on Sunday I chatted with a girl, fifteen, whose T-shirt slogan read ALL IN GOOD TIME. She said she and another girl in search of work had walked five days through jungle to reach Cantagalo.

The midday heat was suffocating. I accompanied four young women through the forest to a river. They splashed cool water on legs ulcerated and scarred with insect bites. One, bemoaning unrequited love, slashed her own hand with a piece of a broken bottle. She sat watching her blood drip into clear water that would eventually reach the Amazon and the sea, unless it evaporated on its way and rained down upon another place in Amazonia.

Only one-fifth of the rainwater that falls into the Amazon Basin flows out the mouth of the river. Most of it evaporates and is recycled into clouds. The heaviest rains fall in the northwest quadrant, an almost uninhabited region of engulfed forests drained by the Rio Negro, a tributary so black it seems to have poured from a moonless midnight. Ten miles wide in some places and 300 feet deep in others, the Rio Negro delivers the largest volume of water of any river on earth except the Amazon itself, which it joins just below Manaus, Brazil, in the heart of the continent.

Whenever I traveled the 650-mile Rio Negro by boat or floatplane, I had to send fuel ahead to be held for me at small riverside settlements. The settlements were thriving missions centuries ago when the region was full of Indians. Slave raids and disease carried most of them away, and now the waterway is so thinly populated that one man, who hunts wild boar for a living, has a lovely mile-long island with glistening white-sand beaches all to himself and his family. The next five islands are vacant, with occasionally an itinerant canoeist to admire wild orchids that bloom in the trees. Surfacing porpoises create small ripples of sherry—the color of the water when seen in a glass. Slightly acidic, it is free of mosquitoes.

The Rio Negro is born of two rivers: the Guainía, with headwaters in

Colombia, and the Casiquiare, out of Venezuela. The Casiquiare drains part of the mighty Orinoco into the Amazon system. This curiosity was put on the map by Alexander von Humboldt in 1800. To retrace his expedition, I voyaged up the Rio Negro in a cabin cruiser with five other Americans in 1982.

It was high water. At nightfall we moored to the crowns of sunken trees and fell asleep to the pipe-organ bellowing of a million ardent frogs. At daybreak we awoke to the basso profundo voices of howler monkey troops, who greet the sun with growls and announce approaching cloudbursts with bloodcurdling roars. They sound almost as threatening as the evening thunderbolts and the crashing of orchid-laden branches split from trees by lightning or gusts of wind.

When we sailed out of Brazil and into Venezuela through the back door, the frontier guards at San Carlos del Rio Negro issued us a *salvoconducto*— a "safe conduct" permit. We steered eastward into Humboldt's "lost world of the Casiquiare," where he heard Indians call meteors "urine of the stars" and the morning dew "spittle of the stars." Centuries ago, wrote Humboldt, this was thought to be "the classical soil of fable and fairy visions," of people with the heads of dogs, one eye in their foreheads, or their mouths below their stomachs. By a mythical lake rose a golden city ruled by El Dorado, the Gilded Man.

But Humboldt found only a few unhappy humans who spent most of their bleak lives slapping at merciless mosquitoes. Thick vegetation, alive with wasps' nests, overhung the riverbank and denied him access to the shore along most of the Casiquiare's 200 miles. For us, it was unchanged, and we even asked the same question Humboldt uttered in despair: With so few people to feed upon, how could so many famished insects know to lie in wait for us on the Casiquiare?

By turning right upon emerging from the Casiquiare, we could have sailed toward the source of the Orinoco. But the headwater region, inhabited by hostile Yanomami Indians, was off limits by government edict. We turned left, down the Orinoco. We planned to cruise 1,200 miles more to reach the sea and complete a circumnavigation of the Guiana Highlands, a corner of northeastern South America twice the size of Texas.

At the Great Cataracts of the Orinoco our cruiser would have to be portaged sixty-two kilometers by truck. But before we got there, the frontier guards changed their minds about our *salvoconducto*. They seized us at gunpoint and escorted us to Puerto Ayacucho, capital of Amazonas Territory, where the governor had encouraged the posting of large anti-American signs on street corners. Charged with "unauthorized entry," three of the other five Americans and I were confined in a six-by-nine-foot cell, which lacked even a bucket.

We sweated on foul mattresses, listened to the cursing of drunks and the slamming of steel doors, and hoarded scraps of paper to scribble notes. During those jailhouse nights I was thankful for downpours that cooled the air and hammered the sheet-metal roof, drowning out all other sounds, even sobs and screams. I would reach out through the window bars and fill my cup with rainwater.

On the ninth day a friendly doctor slipped a message to a local schoolteacher who alerted the United States embassy in Caracas. Although our captors transferred us to a command post 300 miles away, the embassy found us and sent a rescue plane emblazoned with the Stars and Stripes and manned by beribboned U.S. Army, Navy, and Air Force attachés. When they poured champagne at the embassy compound in Caracas, I remembered my jailhouse cup of

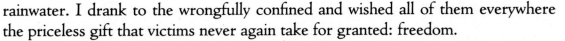

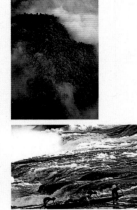

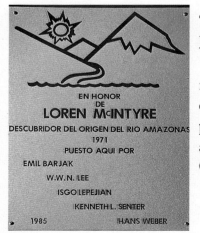

rainwater. I drank to the wrongfully confined and wished all of them everywhere the priceless gift that victims never again take for granted: freedom.

Winds move atmosphere loaded with countless megatons of moisture across the Amazon basin from east to west. Clouds strike the rampart of the Andes at the western edge of South America and rise into cooler air where their vapor condenses into rain. Torrents plunge down the eastern watershed, creating magnificent waterfalls and dense tangles of foliage, which clog the slopes from 10,000 feet on down to the flatland where the rivers widen and lose force.

Laden with Andean silt, these brown tributaries from the west are the most distant headwaters. For many years I had wondered which of the various Amazon "sources" given on maps might be correct. In 1971 *National Geographic* sponsored an expedition that enabled me to disregard all of them and to discover the ultimate source—the one farthest from the mouth.

I worked with the *Geographic*'s cartographers, with stereoscopic photographs made by U.S. Air Force mapping wings, with Peru's Instituto Geográfico Militar, and with the Interamerican Geodetic Survey associated with the U.S. Army Corps of Engineers. We observed that previous expeditions sooner or later went astray by turning up a larger fork of the river instead of pursuing the longest branch. We agreed to trace the most distant feeder rivulet, and to disregard relative volume, since rain may cause one tributary to rise while another falls, and flow has never been systematically measured in the upper Amazon.

In September I set out for the headwaters of the Río Apurimac in the southern highlands of Peru. The Apurimac is a tributary of the Río Ucayali, which joins the Marañón to form the Amazon. My goal was the Mismi massif at the southern margin of a catch basin shaped by a great loop in the continental divide. Runoff from the inner rim of the basin gathers to form the Apurimac, and flows north to the Amazon mainstream.

My companions on the final climb to pinpoint the source were Richard Bradshaw, British metallurgist and mountaineer, and Victor Tupa, the Peruvian director of the Interamerican Geodetic Survey field parties that verify place names. We trudged slowly to the rocky crest of the continent, where at 18,200 feet a breath of air holds only half as much oxygen as at sea level.

On 15 October 1971, we planted flags of our three nations on a summit that Indians call *Choquecoráo,* the "Golden Sling." A thousand feet below us lay a pond that appeared to be the origin of Carhuasanta brook, the ultimate source of the mightiest of rivers.

As the IAGS authority for nomenclature on Peruvian maps, Victor Tupa named the little lake after me when he got back to headquarters, and Laguna McIntyre began to appear on maps in books and magazines.

During the next fourteen years, three expeditions—from South Africa, France (that of Jean-Michel Cousteau), and Poland—followed mine. One day I learned about another ascent to the source by Americans I had never met. A package came in the mail from the Adventurers Club of Los Angeles. It contained a gold-plated plaque, *left,* mounted on mahogany and captioned, "A Replica of the Original Plaque which stands at 16,700' in the Peruvian Andes."

The misty Casiquiare, *above,* is the most unusual source of the Amazon. An offshoot of the Orinoco, it meanders 200 miles through Venezuela to join another river out of Colombia and flow into Brazil. Alexander von Humboldt imagined that this unique link between two major river systems would become a great commercial crossroads. It did not; fewer people live here now than when the baron passed this way in 1800.

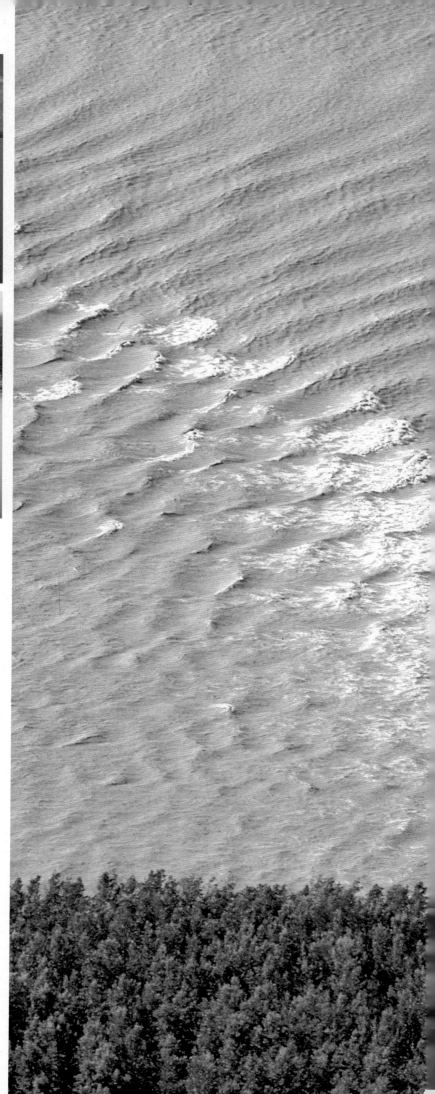

Challenging the Amazon's might, an oceanic tidal wave thunders upstream against the river's current, forming a single crest twelve feet tall, *top.* The tidal bore, or *pororoca* (big roar), can form only in shallow mouths of the river when its volume is slight and flow tides are strong. Reverberation of the *pororoca* against the shores of Caviana Island produces wave patterns, *right,* that leave in their wake a shoreline strewn with the uprooted edge of the rain forest, *above.*

o v e r l e a f
Oxbow lakes reveal changing courses in the history of the Rio Purús, a major Amazon tributary, seen from a plane five miles high in 1949. When I returned in 1976, I could not find this place; during the intervening quarter century the river had cut many new channels while working its way toward the mainstream.

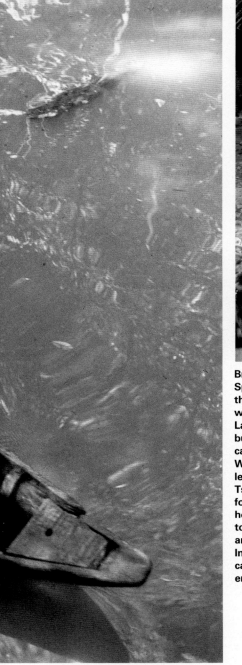

Brazil's *pirarucú* (*paiche,* in Spanish), the principal food fish of the Amazon mainstream, may weigh 200 pounds or more, *left.* Larger and more fearsome are the bull shark and the *piraiba,* a catfish capable of swallowing children. Wrestling a giant anaconda, *above,* legendary Amazon trader Mike Tsalickis performs his famous stunt for the last time. "Never again," he swore, after six helpers rushed to unwind the reptile's coils and save Mike from suffocation. In Peru, *below left,* a well-fed captive anaconda became sluggish enough for a boy to ride.

Draining a region of enormous rainfall, the Rio Negro shows its true colors when water stained by decaying vegetation flows over a white sand bar, *below left.* A mile-wide spiral of dark water marks the meeting of the Rio Xingú with the Amazon, whose brown water carries sediment eroded from the Andes, *below right.*

The largest river on earth after the Amazon itself, the Rio Negro measures twelve miles wide at the maze named Archipielago das Anavalhanas, *above.* A lone chapel on an island, *below left,* echoes bygone days when priests baptized thousands of Indians and denounced slave raids. Most of the new converts, however, died of European and African diseases. The Rio Negro, a black-water tributary, mixes with the mainstream below Manaus, a city of one million inhabitants, *below right.*

Egrets neared extinction around 1900 when aigrettes, the snowy feathers of the great white herons, *above,* became the favored plumage of Oriental potentates and milliners. Fashions change; few women today wear feathered hats and the tall birds beautify tropical forests and plains. And, as the century ends, the Waurá warriors, *opposite above,* coiffured with *urucú,* are abandoning ceremonial use of the red vegetable paste in favor of cheap baseball caps.

o v e r l e a f
Tauarauanã, a Xingú ritual dance, was first described by the German explorer Karl von den Steinen in 1894. The girl, *left,* marks time with her feet and fingers. The man's headdress, *right,* is identical to those sketched by Steinen a century ago.

Circling in search of a gradient tilted seaward, the Río Ucayali of eastern Peru, *above,* drains the most distant snowmelt of the Andes into the Amazon mainstream. A collar of white riverine mussel shells and a belt of terrestrial snail shells are the ceremonial dress of a Waurá warrior, *opposite,* of the upper Xingú River.

o v e r l e a f
Richard Bradshaw took my picture, on 15 October 1971, at the most distant source of the Amazon, 18,200 feet elevation, in Peru. Behind me is Ampato Volcano, and at my feet is the Interamerican Geodetic Survey emblem.

Stranded at the source of the A M A Z O N *... a blizzard at the summit of*
C R I S T Ó B A L   C O L Ó N *... earthquakes, avalanches, and volcanoes ... crossing*
the E Q U A T O R *on glacial ice ... trolling for giant trout in* L A K E
T I T I C A C A *... the demons of Potosí ... with Bolivian*
pranksters at the world's highest mine ... Chilean "castles in
the snow" ... A C O N C A G U A ' S
deadly winds

THE ANDES

The monumental spire of Condoriri, 20,030 feet, *opposite,* accents Bolivia's Cordillera Real (Royal Range), the frozen rim of the basin that holds Lake Titicaca. Beyond the peaks lies the Amazon Basin.

It was dangerous to stay and photograph the source lake of the Amazon while my companions, Victor Tupa and Richard Bradshaw, hurried on down the mountain to our campsite to prepare dinner before dark. The first thing to go wrong at high altitude is judgment: the brain lacks sufficient oxygen. But I had forgotten about that, since the next thing to falter is memory.

I set up a camera on a rock to take pictures of myself sipping the snowmelt waters of the lake whose runoff would flow 4,000 miles before it reached the Atlantic. The lake should be named *Amazonasmayu Puquiococha,* I thought, meaning "source lake of the Amazon" in the descriptive Quechua language spoken by the mountain Indians and by their ancestors, the Incas. They surely found the lake before we did; they were accustomed to the heights.

But I was not. I suddenly felt unable to move on. Bemused by my near collapse—a first in many Andean climbs—I sat and watched the sun go down while my hands and feet grew numb with cold. Belatedly I forced myself to breathe deeply to inject more oxygen into my system. Some strength returned. I remembered that I had not eaten anything since having a cup of steaming Jell-O before dawn. Like many climbers, I seldom seem to get properly hungry or thirsty at high altitudes. I nibbled a chocolate bar and began working my way down the mountain in the dark.

At the foot of the slope, still 16,000 feet above sea level, I floundered into an alpine bog and broke through a crust of ice. I got soaked and chilled but was too weary to recognize how badly off I was.

When I failed to arrive at our campsite for dinner, Victor set a lantern on a rise and Richard headed back uphill, holding his flashlight high. My luck held, the night stayed clear. Soon I spotted both specks of light, yellower than stars, beckoning as warmly to me as if they were neon advertisements for food, lodging, and companionship.

Mountain climbing may teach self-reliance, but it also begets loneliness, a feeling I never learned to like. I started climbing at the age of twelve in the Olympic Mountains—a pure wilderness then—on Seattle's western horizon. At a scout camp on Hood Canal the summer before the start of the Great Depression, I had been given a slab of spruce to carve with lines from a Rudyard Kipling poem,

"The Explorer":

Something hidden. Go and find it.
Go and look behind the Ranges—
Something lost behind the Ranges.
Lost and waiting for you. Go!

I went, often alone when my friends' parents refused to let them go along. One summer I camped ten days between two Olympic peaks, Mount Mystery and Mount Deception, writing pages about the anguish of solitude while waiting for my brother Neil to join me. Those mountains, a thousand times taller than I, seemed colossal then. If a gypsy had told me that I would one day produce motion pictures at twice that elevation in La Paz, Bolivia, and would climb Andean volcanoes three times as high, I would not have gladly paid a penny for such nonsense. Humbled as I was by the vast and lonely reaches of the Olympics, I never dreamed that in South America hundreds of summits too ordinary or too remote to merit a name on the map stand much higher.

Compared to the fifty-mile-long Olympic range, the Andes mountain chain is of cosmic proportions, stretching 5,000 miles along the western side of South America. It was formed by the heavy Pacific Ocean floor thrusting beneath the lighter rock of the mainland and shoving its crumpled edge four miles above sea level. The slow-motion collision causes earthquakes and the friction ignites volcanoes.

The northernmost Andean snow peaks rise just twenty-two miles from sunny Caribbean shores. But the evening that a fellow climber and I drove our ice axes into the summit of Cristóbal Colón, at 18,947 feet the highest point in Colombia, we saw no beaches. Caught by a blizzard, we could hardly see each other, much less the flags we had staked to mark our route. We groped our way down the mountain in a nocturnal whiteout that rendered terrain unrecognizable. We spotted our snowed-in tent at daybreak because our pack mules stood motionless around it like white equine statues guarding an igloo.

Earthquakes abet gravity's everlasting effort to pull down loose rocks and climbers from mountains. One doomsday Sunday afternoon, 31 May 1970, the worst quake in Andean history triggered thousands of landslides and took 60,000 lives. Avalanches buried climbers as much as 400 feet deep in rocks. The quake cracked off part of the 21,830-foot-high north peak of Huascarán, Peru's highest mountain, which towered above the picture-postcard town of Yungay, already destroyed by the shock. Millions of tons of shattered granite and ice plunged two vertical miles into the valley below and entombed Yungay's 18,000 inhabitants.

The air at high altitudes is critically thin and night winds get perilously cold, even at the equator. Cold is a selective killer; it tends to pick off individuals who are least resistant to it. But heat can be a mass murderer when it pours from one of the hundreds of volcanoes in the Andes. One stormy night in 1985, Colombia's Nevado del Ruíz—easy to climb by auto and ski lift—belched hot gas and ash that melted summit ice and snow. A torrent of mud engulfed 23,000 sleeping people in the town of Armero, thirty miles away.

Sangay, in central Equador, has been spewing lava and ash upon its summit snows ever since Western man first sighted it four centuries ago. Its Fujiesque cone is seldom visible through clouds that swirl up from the Amazon

Basin year-round, but twice in a dozen tries I have been able to photograph it from a plane. Blobs of lava shot from Sangay's throat like molten artillery shells, whistled past the plane's open doorway, froze into contorted black stones, and arched back down to crater the snowbanks.

Ecuador's snowcapped volcanoes, each rising in solitary splendor from meadow and forest, remind me of the Cascade Range of western Washington State with one enormous difference: the Ecuadorean summits stand a mile higher. In 1802 when Alexander von Humboldt tried to climb 20,702-foot Chimborazo, Europeans believed it was the highest mountain in the world. In a sense it is. When I reached the wall that stopped Humboldt at 18,200 feet, I had climbed higher than the 29,028-foot top of Mount Everest: the earth's equatorial bulge lifts Chimborazo's summit two miles higher than Mount Everest's if measured from the center of the globe instead of sea level.

One icy April morning, climbing high on Ecuador's Cayambe Volcano, I stepped across the equator from the Southern Hemisphere into the Northern, from autumn into spring. The invisible line intersects glaciers on the mountain's southern flank about one-half a vertical mile below its 18,996-foot summit. Ascending the ice with skilled companions on the rope to arrest my fall in case I stumbled into a crevasse beneath a deceptive covering of snow, I crossed the equator at its highest point on earth.

Several Ecuadorean volcanoes have "blown their tops," as Mount St. Helens in Washington State did recently, opening calderas miles wider than the gaping hole left in St. Helens and even larger than Crater Lake in Oregon. One active peak still preserves its symmetry: 19,347-foot Cotopaxi, part of the landscape of Quito, Ecuador's capital. Cotopaxi's last major eruption, in 1877, did not destroy its cone, but incandescent gas melted its ice cap, releasing catastrophic floods that swept both its Atlantic and its Pacific watersheds.

"When I passed this way I found the country a wilderness," noted Edward Whymper, three years later. Whymper, first conqueror of the Matterhorn, ascended Cotopaxi on warm ash. The ground under the tent he pitched on the crater's rim was still so hot, 110 degrees Fahrenheit, he soon smelled burning rubber. He stayed the night to prove that conditioned humans could survive awhile above 19,000 feet.

Thousands of snowfalls later I found the mountain again layered with massive glaciers, although steam prevents the inside of its huge crater from filling with ice and snow. Cotopaxi's ice grinds slowly and audibly downhill, and during my descent a glacier split like a thunderclap, opening a crevasse the shape of frozen lightning.

Just as Cotopaxi looms over 9,350-foot-high Quito, a triple peak called Illimani lifts even higher above Bolivia's capital, 12,000-foot-high La Paz, the world's loftiest large city. With more than one million inhabitants, it is the only big city on the continent of largely Indian complexion, and that is by default: most of its white privileged class decamped after the great social revolution of 1952. I lived in La Paz for nearly six years with my family, as a U.S. foreign aid adviser, producing films and textbooks for Bolivians.

Although like all Paceños I became acclimatized to oxygen shortage, I never dared to attempt to climb Illimani; in those years I was still recuperating from an attack of hepatitis that had almost finished me off in Peru. I kept a

powerboat at Lake Titicaca, two hours from home, in the lake's bygone days of giant rainbow trout. Trolling before breakfast, my sons, shipmates, and I would catch half a dozen twelve- to eighteen-pounders. Sometimes we packed them in hailstones, such was the summer weather. Our record rainbow weighed twenty-six pounds.

For five years we explored every island and inlet of 3,200-square-mile Titicaca, partly for the joy of adventure and discovery. And partly to find good places to fish, often marked by sprigs of red geraniums floating on little bundles of reeds that Bolivian Indian farmers and fishermen tied to their baited set lines near the shores of the deep lake. If our propellers churned too close to the lines, the Indians fired warning rifle shots at us. At night we anchored among reeds at the Island of the Sun, legendary birthplace of the Incas. By 1962, dynamiting and gill netting had begun to ruin the fishing.

When Titicaca's abundant fresh water brims over, a river carries it southward into an enormous basin 12,000 feet above sea level, the altiplano, which has no outlet to the ocean. An inland sea filled it 15,000 years ago. The sea evaporated, and all that remains of it are shallow saline lakes, pink, blue, and green, and white plains skirting dark volcanoes. Along the southbound road, the population thins out until there is only an occasional hamlet. Then comes the Salar de Uyuni, a 4,000-square-mile sodium chloride plain that looks like polar ice stretching to the horizon. Truckers know the way across the pure white flats, but I never ventured out there alone for fear of plunging into a deep blue well of brine and becoming preserved like a pickle, until some vagrant yet unborn might fish me out to pick my pockets.

The road is indeed a "highway," staying at least half a mile higher than Lhasa, Tibet, along the entire 357 miles between La Paz and Potosí, a mountain town east of the altiplano. Potosí was once the largest and richest as well as the most remote and highest city in the New World. Though well within the tropics, Potosí shivers in the shadow of 15,827-foot Cerro Rico, the "mountain of riches" that yielded billions of dollars' worth of silver to the Spanish Crown. Almost deserted now, the highway once teemed with Indians conscripted to work in the mines, while outbound mule trains carried tons of coins from Potosí's mint to finance Spain's hegemony in Europe. Potosí-bound caravans of llamas bore wine and honey from the warm valleys of Peru. Porters and mules brought luxuries unloaded at the Pacific port of Callao: mirrors from Flanders; paintings from Rome; coral—to cure madness—from Naples; and silks consigned to "Pei-tu-hsi" that had voyaged by galleon across the Pacific Ocean in the annual shipment from Manila to Acapulco.

In 1616, the year Shakespeare and Cervantes died, Potosí numbered perhaps 150,000 inhabitants. Ladies of Potosí wearing Cathay silks danced in ballrooms fitted with fireplaces to fend off the frost at two and one-half miles above sea level. Chroniclers listed 3 doctors, 10 healers, 20 lawyers, 120 prostitutes, 800 gamblers, and 8 fencing schools, where young revolutionaries learned how to kill one another in the streets and torch-lit catacombs.

The silver has played out and the rustle of silk is stilled, but the glottal chatter of woolen-shawled women in the marketplace goes on as before. Vertical shafts now skewer the mineral heart of Cerro Rico, a volcano dead 10 million years. From the shafts radiate twenty miles of tunnels, the mountain's bowels that now yield tin, so base a metal that even the Bolivian plutocrats scorned it — at first.

My guide, Edgar Alanes, escorted me a mile inside the honeycombed peak, where thousands of Indian miners once worked six-day stints, climbing rickety ladders to carry out ore and corpses. We had it easier, plunging 800 feet by elevator to Level Eight, while the temperature soared. Edgar, secretary of the mine safety office, warned, "We can't go deeper; the devil hangs out on Nine. If you get lost and a solitary miner without a face beckons to you from the dark of an unused tunnel, do not obey. Especially if he is dressed as in olden times: no helmet, no lamp, just a torch."

"Doesn't God have a say in here? I thought the devil lives in hell."

"Level Nine is hell enough."

We got out at Eight, exactly one hundred feet above the demonic Nine. The devil must be hard of hearing to endure the head-splitting noise of pneumatic jackhammers. In the confined space at the end of a tunnel, miners stripped to loincloths were drilling holes in solid rock to insert blasting powder. Explosive charges would be detonated at noon while miners lunched inside the mine a safe distance away.

Whenever miners triggered their drills, the vibration showered ore-stained sweat all over my equipment. They frowned at my cameras because photography, like women, is taboo in Bolivia's lofty mines. Both are said to attract *tíos* or *supayas,* mischievous demons who spoil pictures and take advantage of ladies. I foiled the image-smearing *supayas* by keeping my cameras in a case wrapped in blankets with half-full hot-water bottles until ready for use, knowing that humid air condensing on cold equipment can ruin photography. But the *supayas* tricked me. I soon felt too weak to lift the camera to my eye.

I came to all alone in a room spotted with dried blood. In a while a lame dwarf in a white smock brought me coca leaf tea and a soiled aspirin tablet. He explained I was in a sick bay. "Yesterday a miner died in here after the noonday blast on Level Eight. Asphyxiated. The devil picked him out. Today the devil had his eye on you."

But I suspected that carbon monoxide caused my collapse. It impairs red blood cells, which carry oxygen—already in short supply at Potosí's altitude, where every breath contains 30 percent less of the life-giving gas. The paramedic helped me onto a trainload of ore, warning me to lower my head to avoid icicles and the 440-volt trolley line as I sped out of the ancient volcano and into the healing light of the Andean sun, which the Incas worshipped with good reason.

West of Potosí, closer to the Pacific Ocean, volcanoes are newer and rise higher. Aucanquilcha Volcano in Chile supports the loftiest mine I have ever seen or heard of near its 20,276-foot summit—only forty-six feet lower than Alaska's awesome Mount McKinley, the highest in North America. To go directly from sea level to the open-pit sulfur mine with neither an oxygen kit nor the time to adapt to the heights is to risk death from pulmonary or cerebral edema. I rode up from the 12,000-foot altiplano with Bolivian-born miners—pranksters all—in one of the turbo-charged trucks that haul ore. The sulfur used to be delivered long ago by as many as 3,000 pack llamas, a living conveyor belt that looped up and down the mountainside.

Many miners wore frayed suit coats and sun goggles while pounding big yellow rocks into little ones, giving them the look of Sun Belt businessmen fallen on hard times. For me, a lifelong runner, simply walking around at that altitude was like "hitting the wall" in a marathon. The miners watched slyly when I opened my lunchbox and discovered they had slipped a stick of dynamite inside a sandwich bun. When I asked for mustard, they howled.

Like a child's "connect-the-numbered-dots" picture, Chile's northeastern border with Bolivia and Argentina is drawn from crater to crater of volcanoes more than three miles high. Elsewhere in the world peaks this lofty are layered with glacial ice, but here they seldom hold snow all summer long. Ruptured craters are stained with sulfuric yellows and red oxides. With such scant precipitation, mining is possible at the summits. Sandal-clad Incas were able to climb dozens of desolate summits to worship the sun and sacrifice children by exposing them to the cold. Frozen cadavers five centuries old have been uncovered by climbers who thought—until the moment of discovery—that they were the first to scale the heights. The loftiest archaeological site anywhere is Llullaillaco, a volcano 22,057 feet high. It holds pottery fragments, firewood, refuse from fifteenth-century meals, and even a stone corral deep in ancient llama dung near its summit.

The Andean terrain from here to the bottom of the continent at Cape Horn is so rugged and inhospitable that the only way to explore it in one lifetime is by air—although Andean aviation itself has shortened many a lifetime. Winging high with a door or window removed from a light plane for clearer pictures, several times I have been seriously chilled by the subzero windstream. After one six-hour flight beyond Uyuni I had to be carried from a plane at La Paz International Airport, elevation 13,052 feet, with my temperature down to 92 degrees Fahrenheit. An hour in a hot bath fixed that.

Another time, in the lee of 22,310-foot Tupungato, the world's highest active volcano, a 130-knot gale shook my plane and cast cameras and lenses about like dice on a gaming table. Tupungato's turbulence is legendary. A pioneer of Andean aviation, Antoine de Saint Exupéry, described a winter crossing of the Andes around 1929 in his book *Night Flight*. The pilot grazed Tupungato and other "dead castles in the snow" during the airmail run from Santiago to Buenos Aires. "Dusk began to mingle with the air. On a peak ahead, a snow volcano swirled up and, one by one, all the summits grew lambent with gray fire. Then the first gust struck. . . ." The flight ended when the plane, lacking instruments for a safe landing, disappeared into "the eternity that lies beneath a sea of clouds."

In 1972 that eternity engulfed a planeload of Uruguayan rugby players and their friends. Their Santiago-bound Fairchild F–227, far off course and blinded by churning clouds, grazed an unseen crag and tobogganed down a snow slope. Of the forty-five people on board, sixteen athletes survived, living in the wrecked fuselage and eating the flesh of comrades who had been buried in the snow. Two months into their ordeal they sighted a small plane that circled away. I think it was mine; unaware of their plight, I was shooting aerial photographs thereabout that day for a book about the Incas—whose empire included this harsh region south of Santiago. When summer came, two of the survivors made it to civilization and rescuers arrived on the seventieth day.

Just north of Saint Exupéry's pioneer flight path stands the highest mountain in the Western Hemisphere, Argentina's 22,834-foot Aconcagua. It is the tallest volcano on earth, so ancient and eroded that it was long thought not to be one. Treacherous gales bring the chill factor down to minus 100 degrees

Fahrenheit at the summit. Such cold and shortage of oxygen have waylaid scores of climbers lured to Aconcagua's crest by a technically easy ascent. Their remains lie in a local cemetery under weathered markers inscribed in many languages.

In 1973, I joined Argentine mountaineer friends to search for U.S. climbers Janet Johnson and John Cooper, both abandoned a year earlier on the peak by an ill-fated ten-man expedition. It took twelve days to reach and scale the eastern face. Gales buffeted and flattened our tents at night. We muffled our ears and sought sleep on jagged rocks. Miss Johnson's body was not recovered until 1975, but at the foot of a steep glacier we found John Cooper perfectly preserved, lightly dusted with powder snow. He lay staring at the sun only 150 yards short of his expedition's uppermost campsite, where tattered tents, bedding, food, and fuel still awaited his descent from the peak. Though superbly outfitted, he had lost his rope and ice ax. A crampon was missing from one boot.

I opened his diary. The first days had been easy, and he wished his wife, Sandy, and son, Randy, might share the trip. "I'm saving her letter for the summit," he wrote.

At Camp II he had a savage headache. Cerebral edema, I would guess. "Won't be long before it's all over. Very windy and completely exhausted . . . for 2¢ I'd go back."

At Camp III the final entry read, "Supposed to be sheltered from the wind but nowhere is sheltered."

Mrs. Cooper's letter had been opened. Snow began to fall upon the pages as I translated aloud for my friends. It ended, "Keep roped up, and don't forget the crampons, as I don't know how I'd replace you. You are, by far, the best husband and loving one, and really good Dad, in the entire world."

I glanced at my companions. At that great height and in that catalytic cold, tears freeze instantly and fall away like pearls.

Haze veils Andean valleys below peaks, the highest outside Asia, that mark the border of Chile with Argentina, *left.* The region was overrun five centuries ago by Incas who sacrificed unblemished boys and girls to their god, the sun, by exposing them to freezing temperatures on the summits. At festivals, Inca descendants evoke from panpipes the pentatonic melancholia of their ancestral music, *below.*

o v e r l e a f
After Mass on Sunday morning, Colombian women head homeward in Sibundoy, an Indian community at the headwaters of the Río Putumayo on the Amazon side of the Andes. The region once marked the northern limit of the Inca Empire; the people here still call themselves "Ingas."

Corpus Christi processions commence at daybreak in the Andes of southern Peru, *above and opposite.* Pilgrims trek down from glaciers where they have knelt half the night in an ancient rite more pagan than Christian, Qoyllur Riti, Star of the Snow. In Cuzco, *right,* devotees shoulder a massive platform to carry a saint's image from one church to another.

o v e r l e a f
Few people on earth are exposed to as much unfiltered sunlight as this Indian boy, *left,* who lives 15,000 feet above sea level on the slopes of Mt. Ausangate in southern Peru. His face and hands are chapped by the thin, icy air. At a downhill extreme, not far north of the equator in Colombia, the near-naked folded foothills of the Andes, *right,* are almost too hot for human habitation.

Erupting for centuries, the 17,159-foot Sangay in central Ecuador is the most continuously active—yet least visible—of the Andean volcanoes. Clouds drench Sangay year-round with thirty-odd feet of precipitation. A break in 1969 revealed the cone of fire and ice rising out of dense jungle, *above and right.* When missionary pilot David Osterhus flew his plane almost into Sangay's crater, blobs of molten magma sizzled audibly past us, *opposite.* In 1970 the worst earthquake in the history of the Western Hemisphere shattered a peak of Huascarán, Peru's highest mountain, *below right.* An avalanche of granite and ice obliterated Yungay, a town of 18,000 inhabitants.

Wary but unafraid, vicuñas in the Apolobamba Range of northern Bolivia observe the observer, *above.* A fresh snowfall had driven them down from the heights to forage. Wild cousins of the domesticated llama, vicuñas can outrun a jeep at 50 miles per hour. Down the mountainside, *opposite above,* a peasant pries a clod with his *chaqui-taclla,* a foot plow. While his wife advances, overturning the clod as he digs, he will step back, drive the blade deep, and pull the curved handle to unearth another.

Above, a balsa handcrafted of the hollow totora reeds that flourish along the fringes of Lake Titicaca will last a year before becoming waterlogged. *Opposite, Puya raimondi,* the world's largest herb, has a far longer life, 150 years. Its cluster of giant leaves grows on granite, feeding on moisture mainly from the air, and toward the end of its span it grows a stalk nearly thirty feet high. After the stalk shoots out 8,000 blossoms to be fertilized by hummingbirds, the plant dies, and its seed-filled spires are set aflame by Indians to provide fireworks on Midsummer's Eve.
o v e r l e a f
Rays of the rising sun stamp a rainbow on the horizon beyond a fleet of fishing balsas moored on the Bolivian shore of Lake Titicaca.

Illuminated by the altiplano moon, thatched cylindrical houses, *opposite,* shelter Chipaya villagers who believe they are descendants of a people older than the sun. Worshippers of Pacha Mama, the Earth Mother, Chipayas build homes of sod. A farmer, *above,* threshes *quinua,* a high-altitude, high-protein grain. Sod walls block afternoon dust storms that scourge the treeless plain. Cold does not distress barefooted highlanders, *right,* since additional capillaries in their fingers and toes provide better circulation and warmer extremities.

Above, a farmer hurries to teach his son to plant *quinua* at altitudes too high for wheat before a dust storm sends them running for cover. When a miner dies (seldom of old age, but often from alcoholism or the afflictions of altitude and rarified air: enlarged heart, excess red cells, cerebral and pulmonary edema, and perhaps intensified exposure to solar and cosmic radiation), friends bury him on the altiplano and grieve until remembrance dims, *left. Opposite,* a sulfur miner's lens reflects the image of a writer-photographer hardly able to function at the summit of Aucanquilcha, a Chilean peak so high—20, 276 feet—that each breath provides less than half as much oxygen as at sea level.

Where rain is a curiosity ... I N C A - S T Y L E *raft voyages into the*
S O U T H P A C I F I C ... E L N I Ñ O *and the guano*
trade ... the failed fortunes of A T A C A M A ...
the N A Z C A L I N E S *and Maria Reiche ...*
a mirage at land's end ... harvesting
salt with Rita and the
G U A J I R O
nomads

THE DESERTS

The west coast desert of South America, the driest land on earth, lies largely in the torrid zone, but the air is often moist and seldom uncomfortably hot. In Peru, breezes from cool offshore ocean currents whisk beach sands up to the foothills of the Andes, forming dunes as high as a quarter mile, *opposite*.

The desert seldom comes to mind when one speaks of South America, yet along the coasts of Peru and northern Chile rain is a curiosity difficult to explain to children. I lived nearly 5,000 days on those South Pacific shores without seeing lightning, hearing thunder, or needing an umbrella.

The ribbon of aridity stretches from 5 to 30 degrees south latitude along the western edge of the Andean range that blocks the flow of wet air from the Amazon Basin. Every eight to eighty miles a short river cascades down the western slope to wet a green slash across the ribbon of brown. Farms and cities on these narrow oases soak up most of the water before it can reach the sea. When rains cease in the highlands at midyear, lesser streams dry up.

My wife, Sue, and I made our home after World War II in the largest oasis, in Lima, the Peruvian capital founded by Francisco Pizarro in 1535 after his discovery and conquest of the Inca empire. Our house on Avenida Los Incas was covered with the flowering vines that seem to spring from desert soil whenever water touches it. Lima, then a pleasant city of one-half million inhabitants, had a colonial air. Now it is ten times larger, a blight that oozes into the surrounding desert. Lima is inhabited mainly by mestizos whose progenitors were Spanish men and Indian women.

Four blocks from home our sons, Lance and Scott, used to scamper to the summit of an ancient adobe pyramid. There they picked up bits of cloth and mummified human remains that had been preserved since the time of Christ, until grave robbers shoveled them out of dusty tombs. In those days of little smog, the boys, like priests of old, could see east to the Andes and west to the Pacific. The pre-Inca temple no longer exists; developers hauled it away by truckloads in the 1950s to make space for modern housing.

So sterile is the coastal desert that seldom a bug spattered the windshield when we drove our prewar Packard along the Pan American Highway that threads 2,600 sandy miles from Ecuador to central Chile. But beyond the margins of the desert—mountains on one side, ocean on the other—life abounds. After a four-hour climb out of Lima, the Packard would boil across the Andean crest at 16,000-feet elevation and roll a long way down into an Amazon headwater forest noisy with parrots. Over on the ocean side I saw sea lions gulping fish inside rusty

hulls of sunken ships. Since aqualungs were as yet unknown in Peru, I scuba dived with an oxygen escape vest from a wartime German submarine.

The desert is cooled by the Peru (better known as the Humboldt) Current, which flows north from the Antarctic. It curves out to sea from the northern Peruvian coast. Legend holds that Emperor Tupa Inca, master of all the known world, who reigned from 1471 to 1493, built a great fleet of balsa-log rafts and ventured out on the current with 20,000 soldiers. After a year he returned, bringing booty: black people, gold, a metal chair, and the hide and jawbone of a horse.

To test a theory, long thought ludicrous, that South American aborigines could have made transpacific voyages, Norwegian explorer Thor Heyerdahl and five other Scandinavians set forth in 1947 on a balsa-log raft, *Kon Tiki*, to ride the Humboldt Current to Polynesia. All sorts of "experts" predicted that the logs and lashings would soon rot. Every day Peruvian naval officers and I gathered around a Pacific Ocean chart at the naval academy facing Callao Harbor, where *Kon Tiki* was built. We moved a little flag westward along the chart according to position reports radioed from the raft, fearing that our marker would one day stop in mid-ocean to mark the place of the final message.

On the 101st day *Kon Tiki* landed on a coral-reefed island, 4,300 nautical miles away. The fantastic voyage brought fame and wealth to my friend Thor and inspired many imitators. William Willis, a sixty-one-year-old American, rafted alone to Tahiti. He wanted our cat for a mascot; we refused. Such solitude did not strike a responsive chord with Eduard Ingris, a Czech composer who had worked with me on a Peruvian film starring Pilar Pallette—later Mrs. John Wayne. Eduard's raft mates were an Argentine marathon runner, a Dutch sailor, a Czech radio operator, and a young Bolivian woman said to be an Inca princess from Lake Titicaca's Island of the Sun.

The raft crews lived well on seafood. In those days the Humboldt Current's riches, especially anchovy and seabirds, seemed to be inexhaustible. During the three years I sailed with the Peruvian Navy, I used to watch dark acres of cormorants floating upon the ocean swells, diving and gulping frenzied schools of finger-sized anchovy. Endless columns of birds flew past my cruiser's topmasts, bound for offshore islands where they fed their squabs in nests fashioned of excrement stiffened with feathers.

For lack of rainfall to wash it away, some 20 million tons of seabird excrement, or guano, had accumulated on the islands by the early 1800s. When farmers heard that guano increased crop yields, ships of many nations began to carry it away. Deposits 150 feet thick were gradually removed. But for a century, some 90 million birds kept excreting a fresh supply of guano so that the islands reeked of ammonia many miles downwind.

Three sailing ships still worked the guano trade in the late 1940s. Disembarking from one, I blundered into a rookery of cormorants, black jacketed and white breasted, that looked somewhat like penguins. Hordes of the big birds panicked and fled in waves, trampling eggs and squabs. I stood motionless and soon they came waddling back, close enough to be touched.

In the 1950s, despite warnings that the ecological balance of the Humboldt Current would be upset, Peru let fishing boats net enormous amounts of anchovy for factory processing into fish meal for cattle and poultry feed. By

1970 Peru led the world in fishing tonnage while seabirds, starved for anchovy, died by the millions, their carcasses rotting knee-deep on the beaches. Meanwhile, the Humboldt Current was pushed seaward by El Niño, an infrequent counterflow of equatorial water that causes climatic change and is lethal to anchovy.

Recently I boated to rookeries I remembered blanketed with cormorants, pelicans, and other guano birds. I found most of them empty, desolate, with hardly a feather remaining. The Humboldt Current's whales, sea lions, and enormous schools of fish are also less abundant. Peru no longer ranks among the top nations that harvest the sea, and the guano trade is moribund.

Peru lost yet another priceless source of desert fertilizer in the War of the Pacific, fought a century ago with Chile—a war still being waged vocally in wardrooms of the Peruvian Navy. In 1879 Chile seized from Peru and Bolivia the Atacama Desert, whose soil is rich in sodium nitrate, or salitre, then in high demand for fertilizer and in making gunpowder. Since it is processed from minerals soluble in water, the accumulation of salitre, like guano, depends on the absence of rainfall. The Atacama coast is the driest place on earth: rain gauges in the port cities of Iquique and Antofagasta hardly ever register enough precipitation to wet a sheet of paper.

In time the commercial extraction of nitrogen from the atmosphere ruined the Chilean nitrate business. Along the Pan American Highway a traveler passes scores of nitrate factories that gave up the ghost during the Great Depression and are now national monuments called *cementerios*—cemeteries of dead machinery, adobe rubble, and teetering bandstands. Rusty iron smokestacks stand over the industrial tombs, their guy wires humming forlornly in the desert wind.

Saving ancient monuments is an obsession of my old friend Maria Reiche. Maria is devoting her final years to preventing damage to the Nazca Lines that she has long studied in southern Peru. Enormous geometric and zoomorphic designs traced on the desert floor one or two thousand years ago pose a mystery as yet unsolved: why did the Indians create gigantic patterns that can be appreciated only from the air?

I occasionally accompanied Maria on her desert expeditions. While I huddled at night in my sleeping bag on the seat of a pickup truck, Maria would curl up on the sand in a nest of old tape measures, sleeping in the same wool skirt she had worn for months. She rose before dawn to breakfast on unripe grapefruit and canned milk and then resume her everlasting attempt to solve the riddle of the markings by measuring their lengths and azimuths. She scolded me for scuffing pebbles and for pushing aside a weathered red boulder.

"Come on, Maria, there must be a billion rocks like this between here and your hotel in Nazca."

"Is that so? Have you studied its placement relative to other rocks? You musn't destroy possible records of the past."

Born in Dresden, Germany, in 1903, Maria is now blind. Her sister, Renata, lectures at the Hotel Nazca and entertains tourists with tales of Maria's adventures and theories about the meaning of the lines. One day's mail brought letters from a deposed maharaja, a detainee in a Siberian gulag, and an African diplomat. Maria customarily trashes her correspondence, a loss to the world of the absurd.

A European science-fiction author insists the figures are landing fields for spaceships. A German scientist claims they were sites for prehistoric Olympic

Games. A Swiss publisher of art books concludes that the fields—some are a mile long—served for weaving giant tapestries or burial shrouds: Indians shuttled back and forth with huge balls of twine, jumping over and ducking under the warp. Maria was intrigued at first by the possibility that some lines had pointed at the setting sun or stars. Her book *Mystery on the Desert* (Heinrich Fink, Stuttgart, 1968) suggests that the figures may have been "ceremonial pathways" for Indian religious rites that a sky deity might observe. "The Nazca priests believed themselves to be heavenly beings," argued an erudite Peruvian in a British-made TV film. "After eating slices of psychedelic cactus, the ancients dreamed they were flying through the air and looking down on figures drawn in their honor."

After my story about Maria in a 1975 *National Geographic* reached its worldwide membership—then nine million—tourist interest in the Nazca Lines picked up. Air taxis began flying over the figures. Sales of Maria Reiche's book soared. What did Maria do with the income? "I have built a watchtower and set up a corps of motorcycle guards to control vehicles. At last I can stop people from trampling the lines!"

Almost as dry as the Western desert is the northern extremity of South America that juts one hundred miles into the Caribbean Sea: Colombia's Península de la Guajira. Much of it is hard and flat, a natural landing field. Anonymous pilots take off at odd hours with planeloads of cocaine and marijuana destined for the United States. Their associates are said to be given to eliminating strangers bearing cameras who they suspect may be agents of a drug enforcement agency. For fear of being arbitrarily liquidated, I have not visited my Guajiro Indian nomad friends for a long time.

In a gentler year I journeyed by jeep to the uttermost cape of the Guajira, Punta Gallinas. Beyond a beach strewn with great sea-turtle shells and dessicated shark jaws, a lone lighthouse stood in the stiff trade winds that ruffle the Caribbean. Its keeper was ten-year-old Rita Worrillú, whose sole companion was a pet rabbit. Her father had gone fishing days before and left the child in charge of the land's end.

Many Guajiras are called Rita; real names are private and can be uttered only by one's mother's immediate family. Rita was dressed in a traditional manta, a square-cut, long-sleeved, calico caftan. As it was short and she wore no ring, I judged she had not yet gone through puberty confinement. That would begin with her first menstrual period and last as long as a year. An aunt would crop her hair and give her herbal drinks to make her vomit. By regurgitating her childhood ways, she would shape her adult figure. The aunt would teach her secrets of love and motherhood. After endless dark days of weaving and waiting in a closed shelter, the young woman would emerge wearing an ankle-length manta, a gold necklace, and a ring. She would be called by a new name. She would be reborn.

With Rita and my Guajiro Indian guide, Germán Pushaina, I shared mugs of *újor*, a corn gruel that is the main sustenance of the nomads. Then Germán and I jeeped along the shore of the Spanish Main toward Riohacha, a sun-baked coastal town once plundered by Sir Francis Drake and Sir John Hawkins. Riohacha mothers still discipline their children with a 400-year-old threat, "Be quiet or Drake will eat you!"

At nightfall we neared Cabo de la Vela, a promontory named by Amerigo Vespucci on his second voyage to the New World. Guajiros believe the dead wander thereabout. Germán told me that lights I saw flickering in the desert are nomads lighting trails to Cabo de la Vela. I asked why. "So that spirits of the newly dead can find their way to the cape and not torment their relatives' dreams."

Next day we came upon an old woman emptying a temporary grave. She was dusting bones and tossing them into an urn for ritual interment in a family tomb. I lifted my camera. The woman screamed and flew at me with a pick, demanding money. Germán fended her off. "She says her brother's grave will remain open in your picture; his soul will never rest." Recognizing that I had committed a serious breach of Guajiro etiquette, I dropped my exposed film into the urn and paid five dollars to compensate her for hurt feelings.

We passed enormous mounds of oyster shells, monuments to times past when Guajiro divers unwittingly helped to adorn the throats of European noblewomen with pearls traded for steel knives. Tire tracks seemed to be leading us across hard yellow sand right into the sea. Germán said the shimmer was only a mirage. Sure enough, a donkey caravan paraded upside down in the middle of waves of heat that refracted light as in a melted lens. When we approached, the shimmer disappeared and the caravan got back on its feet.

Our jeep, hung with water jugs and festooned with hitchhiking nomads, arrived after dark at Manaure, a ten-mile expanse of rectangular ponds of seawater that evaporates to form vast pans of maritime salt crystals. The night sparkled with campfires. We prowled from one to another until greeted with cries of *"Antsh pía! Kazáchiki uaré?"* ("You've come! What's new, friend?"). Out of the shadows appeared men of the Epieyú clan I had met a year earlier.

Women touched my arm, asking, "What have you brought me, friend?" I broke out tinned meat, a bolt of bright cloth to fashion mantas, and colored yarn for pompoms to decorate *guayucos,* the aproned G-strings worn by Guajiro men. I gave the gifts to little old Rita Epieyú, custodian of the family's food and finances as well as the family surname in this matrilineal Guajiro society.

Germán had explained the basis for matrilineage. "About one's mother there can be no doubt. It has to be her blood of which a person is made, as that blood is no longer spilled with every moon once the *little little* man is planted by who knows what father. No one carries a father's blood in his body."

The camp lay open to the sky, sheltered from Caribbean trade winds by a levee holding the brine of evaporating seawater. Pots and saddles dangled from limbs of gnarled trees where women rigged our hammocks under the stars.

At 2 A.M. I awoke to find the camp deserted. I ran to the levee. In the light of the cool full moon, thousands of Guajiros had scratched out claims upon two one-hundred-acre cakes of salt. Ankle-deep in brine, they were harvesting salt in eerie silence. Women in unbelted mantas broke the crust with iron-tipped shafts. Tall bare-legged men, wearing red-yarn pompoms that bobbed about their hips, shoveled wet crystals into piles.

I found the Epieyú family far out on the flat. Two men hoisted a 130-pound bag of salt upon Rita's skinny back and adjusted a tumpline upon her forehead. The birdlike grandmother staggered through the brine to empty the bag on the levee. Again and again.

The eastern horizon reddened. The sun emerged and stood an instant on the levee, its heat pouring into the piles of salt. Heading for their hammocks, the Guajiros shouldered their shovels and crossed in front of the burning sphere.

Star dunes created by shifting breezes near Pisco, *left,* and crescent-shaped barchan dunes shaped by steady winds near Paracas, *below left,* are both found in southern Peru. Only from the air, *opposite,* is it possible to grasp the scope of tidal pools in the sands of the Chilean coast; contours formed by wind and wave change color with the time of day and with the tides.

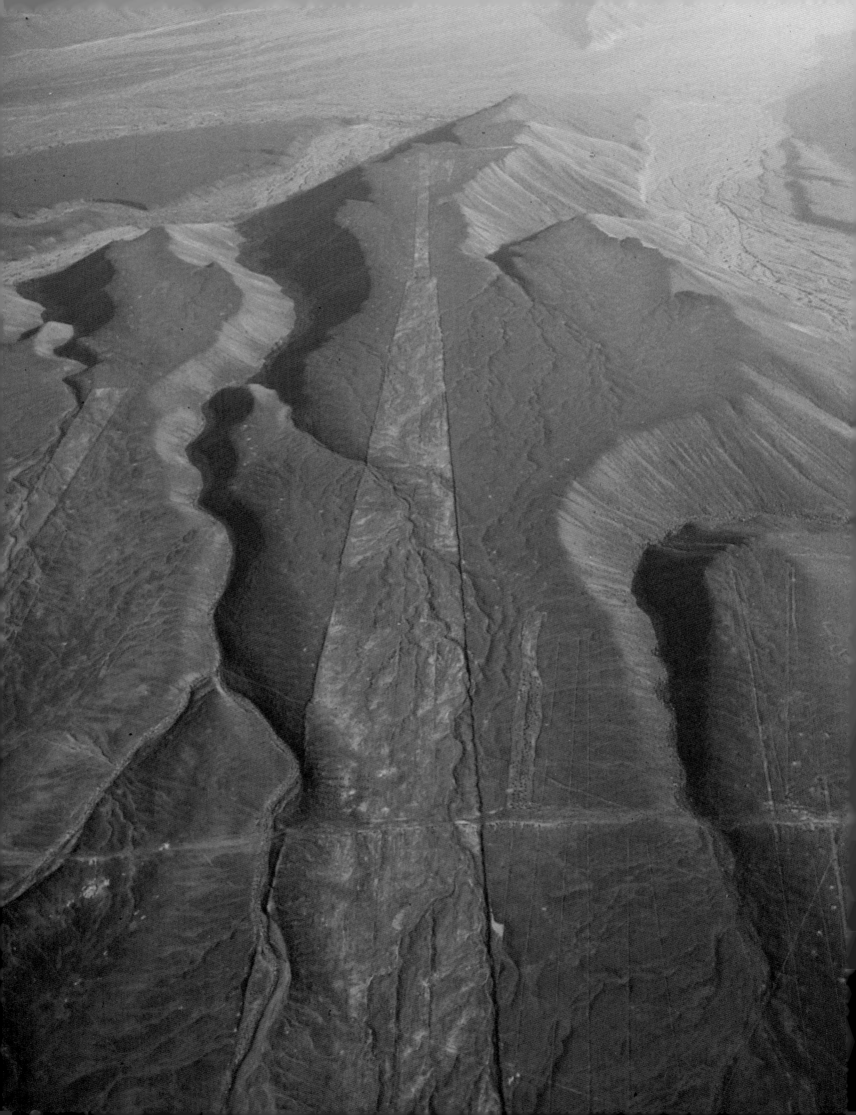

Only man draws straight lines in the desert; the mile-long pattern on a flat hilltop near Palpa, Peru, *opposite,* was traced 1,500 years ago by Indians of the Nazca culture. A 225-foot-long hummingbird on the pampa San José near Nazca, is a zoomorphic example of their earth art, *below right.* Maria Reiche, *right,* has spent most of her life measuring, mapping, and trying to solve the mystery of the markings known as the Nazca Lines: Why did the ancients create enormous geometrical designs and a desert zoo of wildlife that could be clearly seen only from the sky?

Of Brazil's 5,000 miles of beaches, the driest are those of the northeastern bulge. A favorite sport of youngsters in Natal, *above left,* is skimming wet sands on small boards. Fishermen of Fortaleza, *above right,* steer their *jangada,* a sailing raft, into a South Atlantic sunrise. *Opposite,* in Ecuador, at the northern end of the west coast desert, ceiba trees are laden with pods of kapok, a silky fiber used to fill mattresses and life jackets.

In a mirage conjured out of the air
above the heat-stricken sand,
a caravan of women is seen riding
donkeys both right-side up and
upside down across Colombia's
Guajira, a desert peninsula
jutting into the Caribbean Sea,
opposite above. Roseate spoonbills
feed in mangrove marshes near
the Guajira shore, *above.*

The only desert nomads of South America, Guajiro Indians journey twice a year to harvest salt at Manaure, Colombia. Women tote the 130-pound bags of sun-dried salt to the levee, *right.* At the northernmost tip of South America, ten-year-old Rita Worrillú, *below,* waits on the Caribbean shore for her father to return from a several-day fishing trip, a pet rabbit her sole companion.

Sailing through a sea of grass ... tales of B U E N O S   A I R E S *...*
strange feasts of the P A M P A S *... riding with gauchos, vaqueiros,*
and llaneros ... B A R Ó N   V O N   H U M B O L D T
shocked by electric eels ... capturing
C A I M A N S *by dugout*
at night

THE GRASSLANDS

Ships on the horizon seemed to wander at will through meadowlands, their funnels drawing smudges on the sky. Cruising the Paraná River as it meandered across the pampa, we too were steaming through a sea of tall grass. The Argentine river pilot called out a compass course for me to steer by, *"Cero nueve cero!"* "Zero nine zero," I answered, spinning the ship's wheel to turn around a bend.

It was 1935. My ship, SS *West Notus,* was descending a river much smaller than the Amazon, hardly Mississippi-size. We had sailed from Rosario, Argentina, an inland city that led the entire world in grain exports those days. We were bound for B.A., Buenos Aires, the metropolis at the mouth of the river, 200 miles downstream.

I tapped my toes to the tango beat of "La Cumparsita," piped from the ship's radio for the nth time. Carlos Gardel, the singing idol of the tango, had just perished in a plane crash. The ship's pilot, his lip aquiver, bellowed the next change of course as if to conceal the grief in his voice. All Argentina was in mourning.

People wept in B.A., the European-like capital where one-third of all Argentinians live. Slick-haired *compadritos* smoked away nostalgic nights in vast tango dance halls. The *compadritos,* urban dudes, wore tight-fitting black suits, highly polished shoes, and stared with insolence at almost anything in skirts. Wet-eyed tenors bemoaned betrayal and unrequited love, emulating Gardel. Gardel is still idolized half a century later as I write; B.A. is as hooked as Hollywood on past peacockery. Item: every day a red carnation is laid at the bronze feet of a statue of Luis Angel Firpo, "The Wild Bull of the Pampas" knocked out by Jack Dempsey in Reno, Nevada, in 1923.

I recognized that the city was more cosmopolitan than San Francisco, where I had signed on for my 1935 voyage. Many *porteños*—the people of the seaport—spoke three or four languages. But so few could manage English in those days that I still remember a used-book vendor in Calle Florida who had learned English while working for the British-run railroad. He was vastly more worldly than I—intellectually, if not travelwise. Whereas I could drop names like Manila, Hong Kong, Shanghai, Dairen, Port Arthur, Nagoya, Osaka, and other Asian ports I had sailed to before my eighteenth birthday, he could have chatted with me about masters of literature in their native languages—Spanish, Italian, French, or

Rounding up water buffalo is an amphibious operation in the inundated grasslands of Marajó, a large island in the Amazon delta, *opposite.* Brazilian *vaqueiros* separate cows from the herd and drive them toward milking pens.

German—had I been able to. Especially Italian—nearly half of the inhabitants of Buenos Aires have Italian surnames. When Spanish rule ended 160 years ago, many northern Italians shipped out for Argentina, the cornucopia-shaped country below the Tropic of Capricorn.

By 1955 I spoke Spanish easily. That helped me get into and out of some narrow circumstances when, shooting for CBS–TV, I was the only American newsman in Buenos Aires to film the overthrow of dictator Juan Perón. The tightest spot was the night that security forces brought up Sherman tanks and demolished the headquarters of the Alianza Libertadora Nacional at the corner of San Martín and Corrientes. Inside, hundreds of Peronista armed bullies perished. I was in an adjacent building with a telephone line open to New York. Knowing the nuances of the language helped me sort out alliances and enmities in the big city during the anarchy of revolution.

Now that English has become the preeminent world language, many of B.A.'s 10 million inhabitants speak it. Buenos Aires is almost a nation unto itself. It is Paris, it is Rome, it is Madrid. "It is all of Western culture," according to Jorge Luis Borges, the celebrated author I met one day in Plaza San Martín. He wore black. To shake hands with him was to knead dough with caution. We went around the corner to his apartment where his nonagenarian mother lay facing the wall in a room suffused with yellow light. The closet where Borges slept had no lamp; he was nearly as blind as Homer. As we talked, Borges's imagination wandered across mysterious folds of time as in his tales of tantalizing myth and reality reflected in mirrors.

Buenos Aires owed its growth to raising Old World cattle and grain on the amazingly fertile pampa. Native mammalian monsters were still grazing that grassland shortly before the discovery of America. In an Argentine museum I saw a giant skeleton with flesh still stuck to its armored skull and spine. The remains belonged to a doedicurus, a bizarre behemoth with a bone-plated body six feet in diameter and a huge spiked club at the end of its tail. The doedicurus had been killed and eaten by the early explorers of the pampa: American Indian descendants of immigrants from Asia who invaded the continent at least 10,000 years ago.

The Indians also killed and devoured the first European explorers. A would-be conquistador, Juan de Solís, disembarked on the treeless shore in 1516 to take possession for Spain. The local residents feasted on Solís and seven comrades within sight of their shipmates, who promptly hoisted sail.

Explorers tended to lose their way in grass eight feet tall. Not until late in the sixteenth century did Spanish Americans begin to settle on the pampa. Some of their cattle escaped into the grasslands. By the time Charles Darwin traveled the pampa in 1833, wild cattle had multiplied to at least 40 million head, while "wild" Indians were being systematically exterminated by the government.

The cattle were slaughtered for their hides by gauchos, part-Indian cowboys who chased them at full gallop and slit their hamstrings with curved-blade lances. Although the gaucho enjoyed the prestige of being a mounted man and looms large in Argentine literature, he was a *señor de nada,* a lord of nothing but a monotonous sea of grass. He consumed several pounds of beef a day and little else besides an infusion of grass, *yerba mate,* sucked from a gourd through a silver tube. He scorned the six-gun; his weapon and eating iron was the *facón,* a dagger worn at the small of the back, tucked under a broad belt. Out on the pampa his bed was

a fleece-lined saddle. He kept his woman in a hide-walled hovel and saw her seldom.

The invention of barbed wire a century ago began to put an end to the open range. Long before I first traveled the pampa and learned to gorge on slabs of beef served on yard-long platters, cattle had been fenced in and gauchos for the most part had become the stuff of folklore and dance ensembles.

Yet far up the Paraná River I have seen genuine gauchos driving cattle, old-timers splashing through the grassy wetlands of the Argentine Chaco. There, and farther north in the dust-dry Paraguayan Chaco, the fastest gallopers are rheas: South American ostriches about five feet tall. Horses cannot overtake them in a short run. Sometimes riders shoot them—just for fun I suppose, since fast gallopers make tough meat. Rheas have been hunted nearly to extinction.

So have jaguars, for another reason—their pelts are coveted. The great spotted cats are hard to see in grass as tall as a rider's head. I have accompanied hunters who tracked jaguars with hounds in the Beni, the unfenced savanna of northern Bolivia. Years ago hunting jaguars was a test of manhood. I suppose I failed the test, since I shot them only with a camera. Nowadays, conservationists abhor killing them. *Vaqueros* responsible for herding cattle do not share their concern.

Vaquero (from *vaca*, cow) is Spanish for cowboy. In Colombia and Venezuela, however, cowboys are called *llaneros*, horsemen of the *llanos*—grasslands the size of California that curve across the northern reaches of the continent between the Andes and the Orinoco River. Hard-riding *llaneros* formed Simón Bolívar's cavalry when he overthrew Spanish rule in the 1820s. Bolívar's failure to unite South America was foretold by the *llaneros'* creed of freedom: *Sobre mi caballo, sólo yo, y sobre mi, sólo mi sombrero* ("Over my horse, only I, and over me, only my hat"). As independent as a *llanero*, each country went its own way after the revolution.

The first horsemen to explore the *llanos* were German conquistadores whose patrons had loaned vast sums to Spain. Each on his own expedition, Georg Hohermuth, Nicolaus Federmann, and Philip von Hutten searched for gold in the 1530s and perhaps got wind of *El Dorado*, a mythical Gilded Man, and his mystical realm. They found only hunger and death. Some 270 years passed before the crown allowed another foreigner into that part of the realm: Baron Alexander von Humboldt, a Prussian naturalist who would become the father of modern geography and—except for Napoleon—the best-known European of his time.

While preparing a book about the baron's five-year sojourn in South America and Mexico, *Die amerikanische Reise, Auf den Spuren Alexander v. Humboldts,* GEO im Verlag, Hamburg, 1982, I traced his footsteps across the *llanos*. In 1800, his thirty-first year, Humboldt traveled the plains on his way to and from exploration of the upper Orinoco River. To escape the blistering sun and wind, he rode under the stars. One day he sighted in the shimmering distance shapes like masts of ships' hulls down on the horizon. They proved to be the tall trunks of mauritia palms stripped of foliage by high winds. As he found no tree big enough to provide shade, he stuffed his hat with leaves to avoid sunstroke.

Humboldt had begun to dread, as I did on a *llanos* trek in 1978, "the dreary landscape, the ever-receding horizon with its lonely palms which we despair of reaching," when he came to the town of Calabozo. The name, which means dungeon, was well-suited to a place where jails were so full, and hangmen so few, that it was the custom to pardon one criminal so that he might execute his cellmates.

The baron set out to study electric eels in a pond nearby. (Fascinated by "animal electricity" before volts and amperes yet were known, he had already published a two-volume treatise summarizing 4,000 organic experiments during which he had shocked and burned himself badly.) Indians drove thirty half-wild horses into the pond to rouse the eels from the muddy bottom. They slithered to the surface like snakes. Olive green with orange spots, the creatures are really fish about five feet long, with an anus behind the throat and an enormous tail of spongy inedible flesh highly charged with electricity. The eels fired 650-volt shocks into the horses' bellies.

"Foaming at the mouth and with their manes standing on end, the horses reared and tried to escape," recorded Humboldt. "Indians drove them back into the pond where two drowned. Others fell onto the shore, their limbs benumbed." When the fish ran out of energy, Indians harpooned five of them.

Then and there at the water's edge, before the eels decomposed in the heat, Humboldt pinched, prodded, poked, and probed them with all sorts of instruments, even bare hands. "I never received a more dreadful shock from a Leyden jar than that from stepping on an electric eel just taken from the water. The rest of the day I felt violent pain in almost every joint." When the amazing report of his struggle with the lethal electric fish was later circulated in Europe, it won fame for the romantic young baron traveling in a far country.

The flatlands are flooded and green in the rainy season, June to October. "But in the dry season," wrote Humboldt, "grass becomes powder, the earth cracks, and crocodiles remain buried in dried mud until the first showers of spring end their lethargy." Humboldt's host was awakened one night by a caiman that had been hibernating in hard mud under his bunk. Its dry-season sleep disturbed, the reptile erupted from the floor, lashed its tail furiously, and fled.

Caimans are crocodilians of the subclass Archosauria, "ruling reptiles." They have lived on earth 175 million years, a hundred times longer than humankind. When it rains in the *llanos*, caimans emerge into grassy swamps alive with egrets and storks. Some of these latter-day dinosaurs, upon trying to cross the highways that now parallel Humboldt's *llanos* route, fail to cope with the twentieth-century environment: they get run over by trucks. On rain-swept roads I have sometimes had to swerve to avoid smashing into caiman carcasses, though none as big as the twenty-footers Humboldt reported.

I used to hunt the monsters at night. That was in mid-century, before millions of their hides had become purses and shoes, and crocodilians became a threatened species. I searched for them by shining a bright beam along the water's edge until it picked up red reflections from the protruding eyes of a nearly submerged caiman. A pair of coals several inches apart betrayed a broad-skulled whopper. A single glowing coal or a close-set pair denoted a little one.

One night, in a forty-foot dugout paddled quietly by six missionary children, I approached a glowing eyeball fringed by lakeshore reeds. A little one, I thought. Thinking to grab it by the neck and pop it into a gunny sack, I stripped to my swimming trunks, stepped out of the canoe and into the marsh—and sank up to my knees in mud. Only then did I see both of its eyes, a hand's width apart, and a jaw as long as my forearm.

The caiman began to ease backward between my mired legs. To keep its jaw aimed away from me, I pressed my knees against its flanks. It held still, presumably spellbound by the glare of a silent row of flashlights in the canoe.

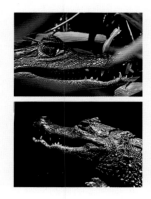

The glare illuminated my plight: I was straddling a six-foot crocodilian —and my feet were stuck in the mud. The children tossed me one end of a rope. I passed it ever so carefully under the belly of the beast. It took forever. The children braced for a tug-of-war. As I tied a knot above its spine, the croc backed up until its jaw was even with my crotch.

I shouted, "Pull!"

In an explosion of spray the youngsters hauled one hundred pounds of jaw-snapping, tail-lashing caiman into the canoe without anyone losing a limb. It scuttled to the bow, where it could not turn around; even so it was a struggle to wire its jaws shut.

Back at the darkened missionary base, we wheeled our lockjawed catch in a coaster wagon to the house of two of the children, where the parents sat reading by the light of a gasoline lantern, waiting up for their return. We jerked open the screen door and threw the croc into the kitchen. It charged across the linoleum and collided with the father's chair, just as he made an Olympian leap to safety on top of the sinkboard.

Their mother quietly put down her Bible. "Please don't bring pets into the house at this time of night."

Two hundred miles up the Paraná River, the city of Rosario, *above,* led the world in exports of grain and beef in 1935, when I first saw it. Its factories processed beef from grasslands of the Chaco, *above right,* the northern reaches of Argentina's 300,000 square miles of pampa. The face of Carlos Gardel, famed Argentine tango singer who died in 1935, appears on the center magazine of a nostalgic collection in a flea market, *right.*

Born on the pampa and reared in the saddle, retired Argentine gaucho Evaristo Cabanelas now wears his cowboy clothes only on Sundays, *left. Opposite above:* Performing at a *vaquejada,* a kind of rodeo of northeastern Brazil, a Brazilian *vaqueiro* rides down a cow by tugging at its tail. An aerial view of corralled cattle on the Argentine pampa, *opposite below,* suggests how the terms "roundup" and "rodeo," from the Spanish *rodear,* to circle, may have originated.

When early explorers searched the *llanos* of Venezuela, *left,* and Colombia for the gold of El Dorado, they overlooked the wealth of wildlife that appears as if by magic when annual rains convert hard pan into lush grassland. Domestic cattle now share the bounty. A young Colombian cowhand, *below,* wears a machete "because it makes me feel like a man."

o v e r l e a f
A cloudburst threatens a herd of cebu cattle in the Colombian *llanos,* the flatlands east of Bogotá.

Storks with nine-foot wingspreads, *Jabiru mycteria,* feed in the Pantanal of Mato Grosso, Brazil, an 89,000-square-mile swampland, *left.* The Great White Heron, or egret, *Egretta alba, below,* lives not only in the Americas, but also in Europe and Africa.

The 650-volt discharges of electric eels, *Electrophorus electricus, far left,* can stun a man. Adult giant caimans, Jacare-acu, *Caiman niger, left,* reach 15 feet in length. The jaguar, *Panthera onca, opposite above,* weighs up to 250 pounds, larger than a leopard but smaller than a lion. Jaguars used to hunt their animal prey everywhere in South America except the very cold regions: the Andean heights and the far south. Then they became the hunted—for their pelts—and are now endangered. So many hides of the black caiman, *Melanosuchus niger, opposite,* were made into shoes and purses in midcentury that the species is now very rare.

overleaf
These jaguar pelts, *left,* numbered among millions of animal hides processed in 1969, when the export of endangered species was still uncontrolled in Brazil. In time, commercial hunting became a federal crime. By 1989 a constitutional assembly had included sweeping environmental protection laws in Brazil's new constitution. The Trans-Amazon Highway that thrust westward through virgin rain forests in 1972, *right,* was soon intersected by penetration roads flanked by farms and sprawling towns. Now almost all of the terrain in this picture has been converted into South America's burgeoning grasslands.

Beneath the R A I N - F O R E S T *canopy ... merciless ants ... ordeal by*
T U C A N D E R A *sting ... gambling a billion dollars on a tree farm*
... uncovering L O S T C I T I E S *in Peruvian cloud forests ...*
attacked by a H O W L E R M O N K E Y *... Jimmy*
Angel's magnificent find ... the
panoply of I G U A Ç U

THE FORESTS

Rainfall seldom ceases in the forests along the equator. When it does, cloud-softened sunlight reveals dense snarls of giant ferns and treetops heavy with epiphytes, *opposite*.

Alongside a footpath deep in a Brazilian rain forest, forever wet with mist from a great waterfall, stands a small green sign:

Floresta é a Cidade Dos Bichos
Não a Destrua
"The forest is the city of the wild creatures.
Don't destroy it."

And like a city it is, a very old city of many-storied woods, inhabited by exuberant life at every level. Were it marked off in rectangles like city blocks, each block would hold hundreds of different kinds of trees, with few alike. Each layer of branches supports a neighborhood of flora and fauna distinct from others above and below. Adaptation to habitation at certain heights evolved through symbiosis of leaf and wing and claw during thousands of years. Other populations are at home on the ground level and beneath it, just as in a city.

The rain-forest roof is an interlocking canopy of many shades of green. Its colorant, chlorophyll, enables solar energy to convert water and air into food to sustain life at all levels—thus counterbalancing, through photosynthesis, the death and decay enacted mainly on the forest floor. The mature tropical forest is not the "lungs of the world," since it neither gives nor takes a preponderance of oxygen; it is a steady state.

Most forest creatures dwell in the unexplored world of the canopy. Bromeliads cup water for them. When a great tree crashes to the ground it disrupts the neighborhood. I learned never to walk along the trunk or among the branches of a recently felled tree lest I be assailed by angry evacuees. The worst is a shiny, black, inch-long ant that travels alone, the tucandera (*isula* in Peru), genus *ponera*, meaning "wretched, wicked, good-for-nothing" in Greek. (Hitting like a hot bullet, a tucandera once stung me in the foot. Agonizing pain inched up my leg. For five hours the misery worsened, nearing my groin. To cheer me up, a woodcutter said adults seldom die of a tucandera sting. "Some Indians pull sleeves full of tucanderas on to boys' arms during manhood rites." He explained in pidgin Portuguese that "the boys have fits and die, then come back to life as men." Six hours after the sting my agony ceased and life was good again, but I didn't feel a bit more manly.)

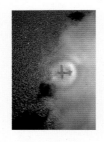

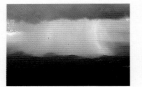

A large fallen tree leaves a hole in the canopy. The space is quickly occupied by younger trees aspiring to lift their leaves sunward. The race, as always in the wild, goes to the swift and the strong. Giants that rise above the rest, the Eiffel Towers and Empire State Buildings of the city of the wild creatures, are called emergents. Forest crowns often burst with crimson, yellow, and lavender blossoms. Extravagantly painted macaws roost there noisily and fly away in pairs. One emergent whose fruit nearly everyone has tasted is the *castanha*, or Brazil nut tree. Never walk under one while its limbs are stirred by wind. Brazil nut pods are hard four-inch globes with nuts arranged inside like orange segments. They weigh perhaps two pounds, and after falling a hundred feet or so, they can shatter a human skull.

Of the hundreds of thousands of forest species, ants are the most conspicuous. Taken all together their weight exceeds that of all other animal life. Ants march from crown to ground with small regard for territory, caste, or tier. The *sauva*, or leaf-cutting ant, is so destructive of crops that Brazilian settlers say, "If we do not destroy the *sauva*, it will destroy Brazil." Leaves that *sauvas* clip from the canopy flutter down as with an autumn breeze. On the ground, the ants scissor the leaves with curved mandibles into disks the size of a nickel and the shape of a gibbous moon. Off they go, in long columns of little green sails—the cuttings they carry pointed fore and aft above their heads. Down into holes they disappear as if sucked into maelstroms. They follow dark tunnels to silage chambers under the forest floor, where leaves are transformed into gray fungus gardens about the size and shape of a human brain. Larvae inhabit and eat the gray matter. Where anteaters thrust their sticky rat-tail tongues a foot or more inside the burrows to feed on thousands of ants every day, *sauvas'* depredations are less noticeable within the forest. Anteaters keep the sylvan *sauva* population under control.

Since the understory of the forest has little growth, at least in the dry season, I can usually slash a path in any direction, counting on a compass or a guide to show the way. Snakes are so few I seldom think about them, but I do hesitate to cross a ravine on a slippery log for fear of falling on gut-piercing snags of logs lying beneath it. I am wary of brushing beneath leaves whose juice I know will blister my skin. When I bend twigs to mark a trail as I pass, I trust none hold fire ants; their bites hurt like cigarette burns. Once a swarm of the tiny red insects strikes, the only relief I know is to run for a river and dive in, piranhas be damned.

But ants are simply nuisances. True danger, as I know it, is not an attack by wild hogs or wild men as presented on TV, but a behind-the-scenes invasion of one's body by microscopic parasites, such as protozoa, that cause fever; fungi that rot nasal tissue; and *stercoricolous* larvae that would have killed me in 1982 had they gotten from my liver to my brain before a Brazilian doctor cured me.

In the wonderfully cool upper air, few germs can reach me. Photographing the forest from a low-flying plane can be like cruising a coral reef in a glass-bottom boat, such are the canopy's nuances of color. The pilot maneuvers around squalls that tower like cosmic toadstools with columns of rain for stems.

Back down on the ground, I have less leeway and less light for photography. My meter says illumination is equal to only 3 percent of noon sunshine in summertime New York. Toward midday, slim shafts of sunlight pierce the rain-forest canopy, spotlighting orchids and mosses, as if a cathedral rose window had let in colored beams to illuminate motes adrift in a darkened nave. But by afternoon, water evaporating from a continental expanse of leaves has turned cumulus clouds into nimbus. Tendrils of wet clouds finger the treetops. My meter now tells me that ambient light has fallen to 1 percent of sunlight. A rhinoceros beetle shaded by a scarlet heliconia blossom reflects too little light to take a meter reading—or a picture without flash.

I set my camera case on a large cut leaf, not on humus, lest it be overrun with ants. A toucan flits closer, out of curiosity. To photograph it I wait beneath a towering cypress whose curved buttresses are more graceful than the masonry props of any gothic church I have ever seen. A thunderbolt splits the gloom. I hear a shattered tree collapse and a raucous chattering of dislodged parrots in flight. Resounding like the lowest note of a pipe organ played in an immense cathedral, a column of rain approaches, driven by the wind. Raindrops begin to spill through the canopy from level to level, pattering as if a thousand worshippers were tapping their fingers against lifted pages of their hymnals. It takes a minute or two for the drops to work down and splash upon my upturned lens.

Rains begin during the final months of the year, then let up six months later throughout most of Amazonia. During the dry season lightning may ignite some tropical forests. Other regions remain inundated so that only a single kind of palm prevails instead of the usual riot of rain-forest species. And man has converted about 1 percent of the natural forest into uniform stands of rubber, eucalyptus, or pulpwood trees.

On a Connecticut-size tract along the Rio Jarí, a tributary that enters the Amazon's north channel near its mouth, nearly half a million acres of virgin forest have been replaced with fast-growing pulpwood trees. Daniel Keith Ludwig, a low-profile billionaire once said to be America's richest man, developed Jarí to meet future demands for paper as a consequence of the world information explosion. Ludwig spent an average of $180,000 a day on Jarí during the thirteen years I watched the project. In Brazil he told me that I was the only one he'd let take his picture since the 1930s. But he is no recluse; I recorded hours of conversation at his homes in Beverly Hills and in New York, where he manages his colossal shipping empire. "I believe you must have luck in the world. And a desire to make things happen. I would never buy gold; it's inert. . . . I always wanted to plant trees like rows of corn. But Jarí is a crap game . . . I'll be lucky to get out of the red in my lifetime." He was born in 1897.

In 1978 I shot the arrival at Jarí of two 30,000-ton leviathans, twenty stories high: a wood-burning power plant and a pulp mill built into barge hulls in Japan and towed halfway around the world. Nothing so immense had ever entered the mouth of the Amazon. Technicians beached them on pilings and connected them to a forestry and manufacturing complex employing 30,000 people.

When high-grade paper-pulp sheets began rolling out of the billion-dollar plant, Ludwig was elated. "Bleeding hearts accuse me of spoiling the fragile Amazon forest. Fragile? Hell's bells, a thousand Jarís would hardly make a dent in it. I'm paying five million a year just to clear jungle that keeps trying to overgrow my plantations."

I remarked that since civilization depends upon paper and print, environmentalists might as well blame Gutenberg.

"Who the hell's Gutenberg? Friend of yours?"

Ludwig's luck ran out when a new government denied him clear title

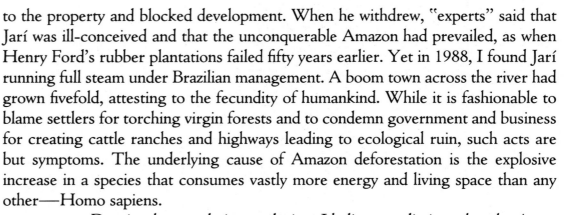

to the property and blocked development. When he withdrew, "experts" said that Jarí was ill-conceived and that the unconquerable Amazon had prevailed, as when Henry Ford's rubber plantations failed fifty years earlier. Yet in 1988, I found Jarí running full steam under Brazilian management. A boom town across the river had grown fivefold, attesting to the fecundity of humankind. While it is fashionable to blame settlers for torching virgin forests and to condemn government and business for creating cattle ranches and highways leading to ecological ruin, such acts are but symptoms. The underlying cause of Amazon deforestation is the explosive increase in a species that consumes vastly more energy and living space than any other—Homo sapiens.

Despite the population explosion, I believe predictions that the Amazon rain forest will be all cut down in this century, or early in the next, are exaggerations. Much of it is too wet. In many reaches of Amazonia high water levels stain tree trunks as much as thirty feet above the ever-sodden flood plain.

Wettest of all is the jungle that greens the eastern wall of the high Andes. Untold hundreds of cascades churn up mists that mingle with blockaded clouds and saturate the cliffs and gulches with moisture. The clouds part now and then to let sunshine perform its photosynthetic sorcery, drawing steep tiers of trees from cracks in rocks and conjuring out of the fog dense snarls of giant ferns and epiphytes. It is a cloud forest, and it hums with insects day and night.

In 1985 I joined American explorer Gene Savoy on an expedition into the cloud forest of northern Peru. Gene had discovered many ancient ruins two decades earlier—including Vilcabamba, the last stronghold of the Incas, destroyed by Spaniards in 1572 and then forgotten. We hired horses and mule skinners to lug our gear 8,000 feet above the eastern palisades of the Marañón gorge. Day after day we slogged up and down muddy trails and clambered over exposed roots of trees and vines, tenting in the rain. Our hired hands kept up campfires and loud banter all night long because they feared that the forested crests, shunned by settlers, were haunted by demons.

The going was often so steep and slippery and barricaded by massive rockfalls that I dismounted and walked with camera in hand. We fanned out to search mountainsides and summits for long-abandoned villages, struggling hand over hand along crags where we often felt almost as enveloped by wet and sticky plants as the fractured rock itself. Gene taught me how to strip moss and ferns from hidden ledges to reveal cut-stone balustrades gripped by tree roots. Little by little he learned that the hilltops held a vast complex of ruins, which he named Gran Vilaya after a nearby river.

I sat among blossoms and hummingbirds taking notes and wondering why the pre-Inca aborigines chose such precipitous, wooded crests on which to build mile after mile of circular dwellings and strongholds. Was the climate drier then so that the ancients did not have to labor mightily to keep the cloud forest from enveloping their cities? The task of clearing the overgrown ruins now would be gargantuan. What happened to the people? Gene did not probe into vestiges of their lives, leaving excavation and consequent discoveries to scientists.

One of the continent's finest, if smallest, cloud forests rises within sight of Maracay, a city an hour's drive west of Caracas, capital of Venezuela. From Maracay a short highway winds over a narrow coastal range and descends to the Caribbean Sea. Maracay stays in view until the highway climbs into the cloud of Henri Pittier National Park. (Heavy rains undermined the pavement on Sunday morning, 6 September 1987. Long sections of the highway plunged into the valley, burying hundreds of Sunday drivers and their families who were bound for the Caribbean beaches of Ocumare.)

I once parked at the lower edge of the forest, intending to record bird calls from the break of day until sunshine touched the high-rise towers of Maracay. The first sound captured on my tape was a diesel truck gunning around a curve. The next, to my amazement, was an uproar of howler monkeys in a nearby tree, answering every screech of rubber on pavement.

The males inflate big echo boxes under their tongues to produce the loudest animal noise in the jungle. I have seldom heard them in the Amazon Basin, except as a distant rumbling. But here a troop was bellowing at passing cars as if protesting the vehicular invasion of their domain. Drivers wheeled blithely along, their radios blaring, oblivious to the rare performance just outside their windows. Perhaps it was just as well no one stopped and got out, since howlers are given to repelling strangers by hurling fresh excrement. The largest primates native to South America except man, howlers live aloft and rarely descend. A riverman in Colombia once shot an infant howler out of a tree. Its mother climbed down, picked up her bleeding baby, and held it out to the startled marksman as if to show him what an awful thing he had done. "Never did hunt a howler again," he declared.

Most wild monkeys get along with people if taken young, but howlers are said to be untamable. David Parry of Turbaco, Colombia, disputed that. For four years he had raised to adulthood a howler monkey named Marco Antonio. Marco played with children and liked to drape his thirty pounds around Mrs. Parry's neck. When I pointed my lens at Marco, David waved me off and cautioned, "Marco doesn't like photographers."

Marco Antonio glowered at me, judging perhaps that David had gestured in self-defense. Or maybe, like tucandera ants and hepatic viruses, he really had it in for me. Marco wasn't in sight when I left the Parrys' country house. But a quarter of a mile beyond their gate he hurtled through the open window of my car and sank his teeth into my shoulder. I enjoy domesticated monkeys; a capuchin has shared my home for twenty years. But show me a tame howler, and I'll show you my scar.

Monkeys are the most abundant mammals of South America's tropical forests, even though enormous numbers of them are killed and eaten, captured for research, or taken as pets. Unlike Old World primates, all have tails—some of them prehensile, serving as a powerful fifth limb. My high-strung capuchin learned to unlock doors and padlocks by simply seeing it done on TV. I have learned enough of her language to communicate somewhat with captive capuchins I encounter in Amazonia. Most monkeys and marmosets live high in the ever-diminishing forest canopy, which is being relentlessly cut back to allow for the advance of humanity. The last primate havens in the wild may be the national forests and parks now being set aside by South American governments.

Some of the tropical forest parks hold the world's most spectacular waterfalls. Angel Falls, twenty times higher than Niagara, was discovered in 1935 by an American soldier of fortune. Jimmy Angel flew into the Guiana Highlands of southeastern Venezuela, sighted a waterfall he rightly judged to be the highest in the world, and named it after himself. From Auyán-Tepuí ("Devil Mountain"),

"Princes of the plant kingdom" is the rank bestowed on palms by the great botanist Linnaeus. The noble trees, *opposite,* provide food and drink, clothing and shelter, car wax, and oil among their bounty.

overleaf
Macaws usually fly in pairs over the forest crown, *left.* Many were carried back to Europe by the discoverers of South America. Early maps naming Brazil the "Land of Parrots" were decorated with paintings of red macaws. The initial drop of Angel Falls, *right,* is exactly half a mile; spray gathers in a rockfall at the bottom to form a second plunge. The total fall, 3,212 feet, is the highest on earth.

a high plateau measuring twelve by twenty miles, Angel Falls plunges 3,21₂ into tropical vegetation. Jet aircraft now fly sightseers past the falls and cliffs almost daily, a dangerous and often visually unrewarding journey through swirling clouds. To reach Angel Falls I had to canoe three days up a swift river flanked by buttes festooned with wisps of waterfalls. Angel's water drops so far that much of it feathers into fine spray which can mist camera lenses many miles downwind.

Even more awesome than Angel Falls are the cataracts of Iguaçu, or Iguazú in Spanish, as wide as three Niagaras and one hundred feet higher. They spill out of forests near the riverine intersection of Brazil, Argentina, and Paraguay. Iguaçu's discoverer, Alvar Núñez Cabeza de Vaca, was penetrating southern Brazil by canoe in 1541 when he saw a cloud of spray rising "two spear throws and more" above the treetops. He had to beach his expedition before it plunged over the brink of an enormous cataract. Cabeza de Vaca was a seasoned explorer. One of four survivors of a 300-man expedition to Florida in 1528, he had wandered eight years in North America, almost to California, as a "naked and unarmed" healer of Indians, and was the first to describe thundering herds of buffalo. But never in his hemispheric travels had the Spaniard seen anything to compare with Iguaçu, the panoply of waterfalls that cascade into a deep gorge bridged by rainbows.

At Iguaçu, nature presents its greatest show in South America. The setting is the forest primeval. Overtures of butterflies usher you through misty green corridors curtained with giant spiderwebs. Waterfalls, one after another, swell in volume as you stroll to the head of the gorge called Devil's Throat, where a deluge thunders. On either side of the gorge, wilderness torrents and trickles play lighter variations on the deluge theme. A week is not time enough to see and hear them all. I have gone to Iguaçu eight times and have taken thousands of pictures, yet I have hardly begun to capture the images freed by the rise and fall of the light and the river, by the waxing and waning of sunshine and rain.

Iguaçu's forests are national parks on both the Brazilian and Argentine sides of the falls. Alongside one footpath in Brazil stands another small green sign:

ARVORE É IGUAL A GENTE
PRECISA DE CARINHO
"TREES ARE LIKE PEOPLE
THEY NEED LOVE."

A shirt of beaten palm bark and
a damaged dugout are among the
few belongings of a Chacobo
Indian in Bolivia, *above.* Denizens
of tropical forests seldom collect
material things or betray
possessiveness, since nothing lasts
in humid climates and residence
is rather nomadic. Leaf-cutting ants,
opposite above, hurry along a
charred log to reach underground
colonies. Fragments of the forest
crown will nourish a fungus garden
upon which the genus *Atta* feeds.
The total ant population of the
tropical forest may outweigh all
other fauna combined. A cock-of-
the-rock, *left,* clears spaces on
the forest floor to perform a mating
dance. Indians trap the valuable
birds by strewing sticky twigs in
the clearings.

Anthuriums of many colors , *left,* grow best in humid glades where sunshine seldom penetrates.

o v e r l e a f
The yard-long macaws are the largest of the parrots. First seen in Europe when Columbus brought back forty of them from the tropical forests of the New World, macaws are noisy, hardy, and long-lived. Scarlet macaws, *Ara macao,* are abundant, although most of the 300 species of these brightly colored birds are endangered by the destruction of their habitat. Many forest Indians keep macaws as pets.

Before its awesome plunge, the Iguazú River fans through the forest, and at the edge of its gorge it splinters into hundreds of cascades, *below.* At sundown thousands of swifts return from hunting insects to circle inside the gorge, *right.* Diving until their speed matches the velocity of the falling water, the swifts zip through the falls and cling to the rocks behind them. Secure from predators, they sleep, nest, lay eggs, and in ways unknown teach their young to fly out of the deluge.

o v e r l e a f
Part of Iguazú's (or Iguaçu, as it is spelled in Portuguese) two-mile-wide array of waterfalls thunders out of the northern Argentine forest into a chasm 237 feet below.

The sulfur-breasted toucan, *Ramphastos piscvorus, top,* inhabits the northern forests. Powerful claws equip the anteater, *Tamandua tetradactyla, center left,* to rip apart termite nests and enemies. The telescopic eyesight of the American king vulture, *Sarcorhamphus papa, center right,* enables it to spot prey at long distances. Although squirrel monkeys, *Saimiri sciurens, above left,* do not have prehensile tails, they leap as far as forty feet in falling trajectories. The sting of a tarantula, such as the five-inch-long *Lycosa raptoria, left,* is sometimes fatal. The blossoming canopy of Brazil's rain forest, *above,* is the habitat of countless species.

The princess' earring, genus *Hibiscus, above,* brighten a dark glade. Red howler monkeys, *Alouatta seniculus, right,* roaring at daybreak or to announce the coming of rain, produce unrivaled animal noise. They are the New World's largest primates, after man. The harlequin beetle, *Acrocinus longimanus, below,* big as a hummingbird, reaches twelve inches with front legs and antenna. A pseudo-scorpion, behind it, lives under its wings and cleans them.

o v e r l e a f
The tropical forest is an atmospheric engine. Most of the rain that falls upon it recirculates as green leaves breathe water vapor back into the sky. Even so, rivers such as Brazil's Tocantins carry enormous amounts of runoff down to the sea.

VI

An URUEU-WAU-WAU *exorcises nightmares ... witnessing a
warriors' victory dance ... hunters from* ASIA—*the first discovery
of* AMERICA ... *Europeans encounter* "NOBLE
SAVAGES" ... *investigating infanticide
in the land of the* MAYORUNA ...
the ALIENS *keep
coming*

THE INDIANS

Kwambr, *opposite,* the son
of an Urueu-Wau-Wau headman,
carries a macaw, totem of the
tribe. His people believe
they are descendants of the
magnificent parrots.

When I awoke, the full moon stood at zenith. Had I heard a cry in the Amazon night? Only embers remained of a campfire built to warm my hammock after sundown. I recalled trekking through the jungle to this hamlet in the Indian-held heart of Rondônia, a Brazilian state south of the Amazon River. The cry—I heard it again.

Blanketed in a hammock on the other side of the embers slept my Brazilian guide. At twenty-five, Mauro was a skilled frontiersman and the only white man who spoke the Urueu-Wau-Wau Indian tongue.

"Mauro!"

He rolled out of his hammock and whispered, "That's Surubím, the eldest son of the headman. He's getting rid of the ghosts that cause nightmares." Mauro inserted a pistol bullet in the large hole in each of his pierced ear lobes and motioned for me to follow him and bring my miniature tape recorder.

"Why the bullets?"

"Amulets. The Indians think they're powerful."

We crept to a moonlit clearing where Surubím, a naked Urueu-Wau-Wau warrior, was pacing back and forth, chanting, brandishing his long bow and a clutch of seven-foot arrows. He drew the empty bow, let the bowstring twang, and shouted. I recorded his four-note chant while Mauro whispered in Portuguese.

"He sings of stalking an enemy. He sights a *seringueiro* carrying a gun." *Seringueiros* are rubber tappers who gather cupfuls of latex bled from wild rubber trees by slashing the bark.

"Surubím draws his bow. The bowstring twangs. The arrow flies. Hear Surubím's cry! The arrow strikes. Hear the *seringueiro*'s cry! He shoots at Surubím. The bullet hits. Surubím falls."

My tape ran out before Surubím finished pacing and chanting. He shook his bow and arrows at the moon overhead and repeated, "*Catú* ['it is good'], *catú, catú.*" Mauro explained that Surubím had sent the ghosts that caused nightmares to the moon.

I trusted Mauro Renato to see that I was not sent to the moon or worse. The Urueu-Wau-Wau trusted him. He worked for FUNAI, the National Indian Foundation, a federal agency in charge of preparing the Indians for the

unwanted arrival of civilization and its diseases. The Urueu-Wau-Wau view as enemies almost all strangers except employees of FUNAI. It had taken years for FUNAI frontiersmen to coax a few of them out of hiding by hanging gifts of knives, axes, scissors, and other technological marvels along hunting trails—knowing that the Indian, once hooked on steel, cannot do without. In 1986 FUNAI's president let me visit the tribe.

We flew by Cessna to a FUNAI post, Alta Lidia, in the central highlands of Rondônia, a splendidly remote region of grasslands and rocky outcrops riddled with caves once occupied by ancient man and now by jaguars. Headwaters gather here and flow into the surrounding forests, eventually reaching the Amazon. Brazilian law has reserved 7,000 square miles of this primeval forest for the Urueu-Wau-Wau—a small and scattered tribe numbering about 350 members.

Indians led us eleven hours on a route as roundabout as any on a treasure map, following hunting trails often invisible to me in the green labyrinth without horizon—a suicidal trek in earlier years. To avoid a fall, I grabbed at a paxiuba tree's barbed above-ground roots—like thorny teepee poles—and gouged new fate and fortune lines into my right palm. Mauro washed away the blood with a green soap squeezed from jungle leaves. An Indian swiftly wove a backpack of palm fronds to help carry my photo gear. We came upon a warrior fallen in the forest, shuddering with malaria. I made him take my chloroquine.

At the hamlet I exchanged gifts with the headman, Moãgana. He gave me a wristlet of carved wooden beads to increase my strength. I still wear it in remembrance of his smile. Mauro said Moãgana had killed only two *civilizados*. He and his warriors wore nothing except boars'-tusk necklaces and strange liana hoops around their waists. Women dressed in little more than necklaces of capybara incisors. As with other Amazonian aborigines, even babies wore wristlets and anklets. In the evening, girls played at putting fireflies in their hair.

The next day I watched warriors perform a victory dance, striding in a circle and blowing enormous flutes to celebrate killing a rubber tapper. At the point where "men return from hunting enemies," women joined and circled arm in arm with them. I am one of the first outsiders ever to witness that secret rite—and probably one of the last, for it is doomed.

Rondônia, a once remote territory recently elevated to statehood, is being riddled with roads and overrun by loggers, miners, rubber tappers, cattlemen, and hordes of settlers—166,000 in 1986 alone. An official map of "killings" during the 1960s and 1970s pinpoints fifty-one incidents of Indian bowmen slaying new-comers—including FUNAI frontiersmen—and twelve known reprisals. Many covert massacres of Indians by gunslingers never get reported. Most vulnerable to Indian attack are *seringueiros*. In order to tap wild rubber trees they cruise the virgin forest alone and often stray onto poorly defined Indian lands. Eight rubber tappers and a logger were slain during the three months I stayed in Rondônia.

The Urueu-Wau-Wau let me photograph victory dances, but when my guide, Buabá, died of snakebite, they kept me away. His mother drew her hammock around herself like a cocoon and wailed day and night. Her lament was echoed from other huts. I had seen that sinewy warrior tote one hundred pounds of wild hog meat many miles without resting. While hunting he had reached for a fallen bird and a snake sank its fangs into his neck. His skin turned strange colors, and he died in agony two days later.

I seldom went on hunts because I would rather live on tasteless manioc root raised and roasted by Indians than kill and eat monkeys and rare birds. Game was plentiful; the Urueu-Wau-Wau, like most Amazonian aborigines, hunt whatever and whenever they need with little conscious concern about conservation. Hunter-gatherers of the Amazon preserve their natural habitat better than technological man mainly because their population density is far less and their per capita consumption of energy for transportation, industry, commerce, agriculture, and housing is nearly nil. Besides, they lack the means—except for fire—of witless mass destruction.

Of the thirty-odd rain-forest tribes I have visited in six countries, Rondônia's Urueu-Wau-Wau are the least influenced by twentieth-century inroads. Even the Chacobos I saw in 1962 in a Bolivian swamp made clothing by pounding tree bark. Not Moãgana's people; as of 1988 they wore no clothes and had not been "pacified"—a euphemism for being coaxed into national life at the lowest level—despite their being surrounded by land-hungry migrants equipped with chain saws and tractors. FUNAI's policy for now (it changes often) is to care for their health and encourage them to hold on to ancestral ways.

My Urueu-Wau-Wau friends, like all full-blooded Indians, are direct descendants of Asians from northern China who wandered unknowingly into the Western Hemisphere through Alaska some 10,000 or 20,000 years ago, maybe more; no one knows. Their ancestors crossed from the old continent to the new on foot at a time when continental ice sheets had taken up so much ocean water that sea levels dropped and shallows emerged, forming an isthmus along the Arctic Circle a thousand miles wide and partly free of ice. The vanguard faced a horizon empty of enemies, rich with game, open all the way to land's end, to Cape Horn.

In time the ice melted, ocean levels rose, and waves lapped the steppes where the Asian immigrants had entered America. Those first Americans were short and small-boned, with scant body and facial hair on their thick bronze skin. Wielding stone-tipped spears honed to penetrate heavy hides, they stalked the Ice Age megafauna with surpassing skill, killing hairy mammoths, mastodons, gigantic bison, sloths as tall as giraffes, lion-size scimitar cats, beavers as big as bears, camels, and even horses. All South American megafauna are now extinct—except the tapir, which grows to 500 pounds, and the elephant seal, up to 8,000 pounds, which comes ashore to mate. The slaughter was for food, and maybe at times for valor, since an Indian hunter seldom seems so elated as when telling about his kill, be it animal or human. Some tribesmen even ate the flesh of vanquished enemies.

Distant descendants of the hunters from Asia reached tropical South America and ranged onward, adapting to Andean heights and glacial cold while exploring the 6-million-square-mile continent. They diversified, but without approaching the variety of appearance and customs of the races spreading over Europe, Asia, and Africa at the same time. Lost voyagers from those other continents may have landed on American shores in forgotten times, as suggested by archaeological finds of Japanese-like relics and long un-Indian beards on effigies, but too few aliens arrived to alter the bloodline. Even today, wherever they live, from Alaska to Tierra del Fuego, pure-blooded Native Americans are relatively easy for anthropologists to recognize.

They came to speak hundreds of different languages, calling themselves not Indians but whatever group name honored their totem or place of

presumed racial origin: Cat People, Cave People, or simply The People. There existed at least a thousand names, a thousand tribes—all of the same race—when Columbus arrived in 1492 and simplified the nomenclature without at all intending to. Columbus believed he had reached the fabled Indies off the coast of China and called the inhabitants Indians. He was mistaken, but a generic name was needed, and once coined, it became currency.

In April 1500 the Portuguese fleet of Pedro Alvares Cabral, blown too far west on a voyage to India, anchored off an unexpected shore. "We caught sight of men walking on the beaches. . . . They were dark and entirely naked, with bows and arrows in hand." Mariners invited natives on board and were fascinated by their nudity, feather headdresses, and body paint of black and red vegetable dyes. Those first Brazilians beheld by Europeans seemed "rather like birds or wild animals, so clean, so plump, and so beautiful. Their innocence is as great as Adam's. . . ."

The following year Amerigo Vespucci felt "near the terrestrial paradise" when sailing the Brazilian coast of the continent which would soon bear his name. Vespucci lived twenty-seven days among the Indians, marveling at the ease of childbirth, their great longevity, and the lack of any concept of private ownership. He rebuked the aborigines for eating slain enemies and declared that "the astonishing thing about their wars and cruelty is that we could find no reason for them, since they have no property or lords or kings or desire for plunder, or lust to rule, which seem to me to be the causes of wars and of disorder."

Such reports by New World discoverers fostered the tradition of a "noble savage" living in harmony with nature. This led to European philosophizing in the eighteenth century—mainly by Jean-Jacques Rousseau—about the natural goodness of humankind, and some of the rights later expressed by Thomas Jefferson in the Declaration of Independence.

As soon as Europeans began to take possession of Indian property in the name of God and distant kings and lay out city streets and fortifications, they found that the Indians' disregard for wealth and material possessions had its drawbacks for colonization: the noble savages refused to work. They loved to hunt but hated to hoe. The magnificent archers fled into the forests or perished in frightful epidemics. The new masters then brought in Africans—better able to survive slavery and more resistant to Old World diseases—who soon outnumbered the aborigines.

The vexation of Western man with the Indians' lack of ambition and indifference to time overflows in an 1854 publication of the U.S. Congress. The writer found it "sad to think that the Amazon is but the dwelling place of the savage and the wild beast since it is capable of supporting in luxury millions of civilized people." He regretted that "Indians cannot bear the restraints of law or the burden of sustained toil," and concluded that "civilization must advance, though it tread on the neck of the savage, or even trample him out of existence."

Pro-Indian voices—of priests and kings, a Holy Roman emperor, benevolent governors, Brazilian poets—have always been raised, but in vain. The tone of nearly all the voices had been patronizing, since each speaker could not help feeling that his own culture, being prevalent, was superior to that of primitives who needed coddling. Nowadays all sorts of agencies "protect" the Indians, some trying to coax them into the mainstream of national life, and others aiming to

isolate Indians from all outside contact, pretending that events from 1492 onward never happened.

In 1977 the *Washington Post* ran a wire-service feature from Brazil reporting that the remote Mayoruna tribe was "killing its babies out of despair at the penetration of its culture by the advance of civilization." I agreed to look into the alleged infanticide for a European periodical, although the story seemed far-fetched since the Mayorunas live far up the Rio Javarí, the meandering border of Brazil and Peru, weeks by canoe from the nearest town and civilization. They had fled into the wilderness a century ago to escape slave raids by other Indians and remained concealed until missionaries contacted a few of them on the Peruvian side of the river in 1969. Prospectors protected by soldiers had searched the Brazilian side for oil from 1972 to 1974 and departed empty-handed—small cause for tribal infanticide. General Ismarth de Araujo Oliveira, then director of FUNAI, told me he believed the story had been faked by a disgruntled ex-employee, and he encouraged me to investigate and form my own opinion. The former FUNAI employee, Paulo Lucena, echoed an argument of European critics who think they understand Indian problems better than Brazilians. He told me, "The agency is ethnocentric and its so-called Statute of the Indian was neither discussed with nor ratified by the Indian." However, Lucena did not suggest how to bring forest Indians—illiterates who speak many different tongues and war on each other—to agree on a law proposed by a government they know nothing about.

"Mayorunas beheaded two FUNAI agents last year," Lucena warned. "Better carry a gun." I preferred to go without.

Leaving the twentieth century behind, my pilot flew two hours from the Amazon up the Javarí, waggled wings above a FUNAI outpost, and well beyond it found a stretch of river free enough of fallen trees to put down his floatplane near a muddy beach. I camped on the riverbank alone for two uneasy days and nights, my hammock slung between trees.

Out of the mist on the third morning came a dugout canoe paddled by Indians wearing long cat whiskers of palm spines inserted into holes in their tattooed lips. Mayorunas. The cougar is the tribe's totem. The FUNAI agent had sent them to fetch me to the post, three days away. I gave my name; one pronounced it "Lowen." His name? *"Não tem,"* he said ("Don't have"). That meant "I won't tell you"; it was taboo to let strangers speak his real name lest he become bewitched. So I called him Roberto. His companions used Brazilian aliases: *Cambio* ("Over" in radio lingo) and *Por Amor de Deus* ("For God's sake").

A name I well remember is Sally Doña Perez, because of the *Doña* ("Lady") oddly placed in the middle of it. The lady is a slave I met on my first day's travel to the FUNAI post. Confined to her hammock, Sally occupied a shadowy corner of a hut concealed in a patch of banana trees on the riverbank. Aging, thin as a famine victim, Sally was crippled with arthritis, cataracts, and goiter. She spoke Spanish—a surprise.

Born in Tarapoto, Peru, Sally was sold to a river trader by her stepfather at age six. "Then a Mayoruna warrior, Siní, captured me and carried me to the east across three rivers. In the Mayoruna fashion, he pierced my nose, tattooed my lips, and raised me to be his bride. I forget how many little ones I brought to light. Nearly all died. One night Kacuá, a powerful Mayoruna, killed Siní and took me to raise a new family on the Brazilian side of the river."

Hollow reed "lipsticks" and fiber ear ornaments adorn the face of a Yanomamö woman, *opposite*, who needs no eye makeup. She belongs to the largest Indian nation still living in the tropical forest wilderness on both sides of the Brazil-Venezuela border.

Sally's story ended as the sun touched treetops to the west. *"Adios, Sally Doña Perez"* ("Good-bye, my lady"). *"Adios, mi caballero"* (Good-bye, kind sir").

We arrived after dark at a hut where an Indian gave up his straw pallet for me. Next morning I saw that his face and torso were covered with pustules and hoped it wasn't smallpox.

After three days on the Javarí we cut our way up a creek through trunks of shallow-rooted trees felled by storms. At FUNAI's Pôsto Lobo, agent Isidro Bautista Silva was waiting, in vain, for things he'd not received in fourteen months, mainly mail and gasoline; money was useless at the post.

A Mayoruna chieftain approached to *trocar presentes:* in exchange for reading glasses to enhance his vision he gave me ankle bindings to improve my stride. I slept without a mosquito net and awoke before daybreak to sounds of Mayorunas drinking water and throwing up, beginning a new day by washing out their stomachs. I translated for Isidro the *Washington Post* article about Mayoruna infanticide while children crowded around us. Would he help take a census?

"In nearby villages, yes, but not distant ones where hostile Mayorunas set alarms and traps in the trails."

We counted families hut by hut. I attracted people outside by demonstrating sailors' knots. Men lounged on logs, women on mats. Minutes have no meaning; wristwatches are simply jewelry with revolving parts. Only Isidro, conditioned like most *civilizados* to respond to a clock inside his head, kept busy, fixing an outboard motor and teaching the three Rs—in his fashion.

Isidro took the census by penciling huts on a brown paper bag and underlining them with Xs and Ys as if he were charting chromosomes. We counted few old folks. Perhaps the elders had concluded, as Indians sometimes do, that their time had come, and they had let themselves expire. But if the tribe had "decided to die," it was not by infanticide. One infant perished while I was there, but from diarrheal dehydration, not murder. Relatives buried him under the floor and sealed the hut. Isidro said some Mayorunas could not bear to let maggots consume their kin: they roast and eat their own dead, lamenting all the while. Of the 325 Mayorunas we counted at villages in the forest, more than 200 were children.

Isidro had ignored one hut, saying a woman lived there but she didn't count because she was a slave named Sinsi. I picked the lock and peeked inside.

In the shadows a light-skinned girl was nursing a baby. Sinsi had a young body, patrician hands, and sorrowful eyes. She didn't object when I raised my camera but refused to look at Polaroid snapshots. The slave girl was the only person I saw who showed the "despair" reported by the press—but she was not a Mayoruna and her baby had not been slain.

When I returned to the clockwork world it was good to report to FUNAI's director, Ismarth, that Mayorunas around Pôsto Lobo were not on the wane. And to learn, by sending a Polaroid to the World Health Organization, that the Indian in whose bed I'd slept only had chickenpox. Smallpox, that greatest annihilator of Indians, has been eradicated.

But a deadlier scourge, the alien human intruder, continues to spread. The last Indian diehard dwellers in the rain forest know they cannot escape "pacification" much longer, for planes spy overhead and no hiding place is secret anymore.

A yellow cock-of-the-rock, *Rupicola rupicola, above,* watches from the shadows as a flight of pierid butterflies, *right,* salutes four Cintas Largas Indian girls kneeling in the Rio Aripuaná, Mato Grosso, Brazil.

Letting fly with astonishing accuracy at a high target (a monkey woven of palm fiber), Txicão warriors, *above,* practice archery at the close of a day spent assembling framework for a house. A few miles away, a Kamayurá dance instructor drills his class, *opposite,* and a brother and sister train their pet macaw to fetch, *opposite above.* Within Xingú National Park's 10,200-square-mile wilderness, thirteen such tribes are watched over by FUNAI, the National Indian Foundation. Xingú Park originated with a crusade in the 1950s and 60s by the Villas Boas brothers, frontiersmen Orlando, Claudio, and Leonardo, to delay the "civilization" of upper Xingú River tribes lest they be decimated by warfare and disease as elsewhere in Brazil. Even so, the Txicão population dropped from 400 to 53 during the 11 years it took the Villas Boas to convince them to declare peace.

Rainbows are associated with snake demons in myths of many tribes. A Txicão Indian of Mato Grosso, *left,* considers which of his long arrows he might let fly to scare one of the pair from the sky. For the Urueu-Wau-Wau warrior with the resplendent headdress, *below,* the sun is a benevolent being, while the moon is a wasteland populated with nightmares that fall upon the earth.

o v e r l e a f
In the forest, an Urueu-Wau-Wau child crosses a gulch on a slippery log bridge, *left.* I tore my hand on the barbed above-ground roots —like thorned teepee poles—of the paxiuba tree at left. In the village, a Kamayura wrestler recovers between bouts, *right.*

A *morerequat,* male chief of the Kamayurá, *above,* smokes a ritual cigar of green tobacco while watching the Tauarauanã. Men adorn their arms with aromatic leaves and leap to the rattle of a maraca and the thump of a small hollow log, *opposite above.* Jakuí flutes, played in threes, *opposite,* symbolize male sexuality and a malevolent spirit who dwells on the bottom of Alto-Xingú waterways. Flutists feel they become the spirit. Women are forbidden to behold the flutes.

In Rondônia's primeval forest, Borobá enjoys bathing in the cool headwaters of the Amazon, *above.* Betrothed since her seventh or eighth year, Borobá cannot read and does not know she is Brazilian, for modern times have not yet penetrated the heartland of her Urueu-Wau-Wau tribe. As with the girl spinning wild cotton, *below right,* Borobá is schooled in both domestic and jungle lore. For her sister, *below far right,* she fashioned a necklace of capybara incisors, badge of femininity. Farther upstream, Moāgana, headman of her hamlet, hunts waterfowl, *right.*

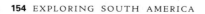

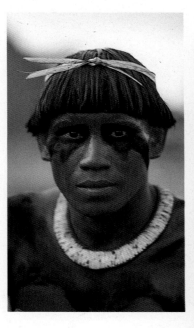

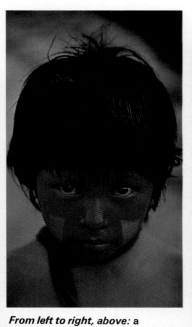

From left to right, above: a Kuikuro dancer of the forested Alto Xingú swamplands; a Mayoruna woman whose "whiskers" identify her tribal totem as the puma; a Txukahaméi girl whose forest home was bisected by Brazil's highway B–80; a Bororo chieftain of a once warlike Mato Grosso tribe; and a Yanomamö boy, *opposite,* whose nation inhabits the Río Orinoco headwaters in Venezuela.

In 1953, on the upper Amazon of Peru, a grass-costumed Yagua youth aims a ten-foot blowgun, *left.* In 1976 an Erigpactsá chief in Mato Grosso, Brazil, *below left,* wears plumes in his pierced septum and balsa-wood disks inserted into the six-inch-diameter holes in his ear lobes. In 1966 sophisticated Gabriel Calazacón, *opposite,* owned 800 head of cattle near Santo Domingo de los Colorados, Ecuador. Gabriel's brother Abrahám, a famous Colorado shaman, treated patients from Europe and the Americas with herbal remedies at his clinic in the rain forest west of the Andes.

Before Europeans arrived, most American aborigines adorned themselves with vegetable dyes. Indians still do in regions where contact with *civilizados* is slight. The Txicão axman, *left,* wore red from head to foot while cutting down a tree in Mato Grosso, Brazil. The Kamayurá bowmen hunting fish in Lake Ipavú, *opposite,* a headwater of Brazil's Xingú River, apply elaborate makeup almost every morning and bathe in the afternoons. Panésh, a Mayoruna bride, *opposite below,* describes how Brazilian petroleum prospectors escorted by troops arrived by helicopter. She lives near the Javarí, a river bordering Brazil and Peru.

o v e r l e a f
Bivouacking at nightfall, headman Moãgana and one of his wives pause on the savannah of Rondônia's central highlands during a trek to their hamlet in the Brazilian rain forest.

VII

Pillaged T O M B S *of pre-Inca states ... the necropolis of* P A R A C A S ...
the Moon Kingdom of Chimor ... treasures of the last secret
E M P I R E *on earth ... finding a* T I M E C A P S U L E
lost in the jungle ... rebuilding a " B R I D G E
O F S A N L U I S R E Y "

LOST EMPIRES

Lured by legends of the buried

wealth of lost empires,

plunderers have ravaged

pre-Columbian graveyards

along the coastal deserts

of Peru for centuries, *opposite.*

We stared aghast at skulls and shattered skeletons that littered the cratered ground, underfoot and all the way to distant hills, as if acres of graves had opened up at doomsday. Long black hair clung to yellow craniums as yet unbleached by the sun. Black tattoos decorated the brittle brown skin of mummified arms.

In 1948 my wife, Sue, and I happened upon a plundered Indian burial ground while seeking a place to picnic in the Chillón River valley, an hour's drive from our home in Lima, Peru. The overturned earth was strewn with fragments of ancient pottery smashed by seekers of buried gold. The only moving thing in that apocalyptic landscape was our three-year-old son, Lance. He had run from our jeep and was picking his way through bones and potsherds and tatters of handwoven cloth that still held color, exclaiming, "Look! Pots lots!"

Sue called him back. He obeyed, and as I pulled away to look for a better picnic place, he shook his finger at the skulls and scolded all those "broken boys who didn't mind their mothers."

When I returned years later I found only a few of the "broken boys." The river had washed away most of the tombs and skeletons sometime in the mid-1970s. It must have been the worst flash flood in a thousand years, as archaeologists had dated many graves at around A.D. 900. The cemetery belonged to one of the rich city-states that arose with the advent of agriculture in riverine oases along the coast of Peru. The graves had remained undisturbed during the city-states' internecine wars and eventual subjugation by the Incas. But with the European conquest of South America in the 1500s, the plundering of tombs began, and it still goes on.

More than a dozen adobe pyramids a city block in size stood around the outskirts of Lima when we moved there in 1947. The once towering temples, long abandoned and weathered, are *huacas*—an Inca word for holy places or things. Objects taken from them are *huacos* and men who dig them up professionally are termed *huaqueros*. The *huacas* were the first relics of ancient civilizations that I photographed from the air in 1972 when the Peruvian Government lent me an observation plane and pilot to seek out archaeological sites along the coast.

South of Lima my pilot circled the ruin of Pachacamac, once the most famous shrine on the Pacific coast of South America. Its oracle had attracted pilgrims centuries before Inca times. After fasting, worshipers walked backward

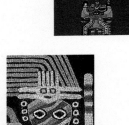

into unlit chambers to consult the oracle and listen to prophecies uttered in hisses, probably by a hidden priest pretending to be a voice from the netherworld.

In the sixteenth century the oracle blundered. When Huayna Capac, the twelfth Inca and last emperor, fell ill in Quito, the oracle sent word by messenger to cure him by exposure to the sun. Wrong—Huayna Capac died. With a huge army, his son Atahuallpa set out from Quito to be ordained emperor in Cuzco, the imperial capital, 1,500 road miles to the south. Atahuallpa paused enroute to inquire about bearded men said to be stepping ashore from floating houses. The Pachacamac oracle advised him not to fear the silver-shirted foreigners; all would perish. Wrong again—the aliens, led by Francisco Pizarro, fell upon Atahuallpa, held him for ransom, then garroted him and went on to seize Cuzco for themselves.

We flew on down the coast to one river oasis after another. I photographed arrays of *huacas* standing in fields of cotton. At every oasis we turned inland and piloted up its life-giving stream until the canyon narrowed and farms thinned out. Many such defiles hold ruins of strongholds built by Inca highlanders to launch attacks on coastal kings.

Near Paracas, 140 miles south of Lima, I flew over the site of a strange kingdom long lost under the desert sand. Rising to power in 500 B.C., the people of Paracas rejoiced in taking human heads for trophies. They spent years of their lives preparing for the death of dignitaries by fashioning elegant garments in which to inter them in the deep, bottle-shaped vaults of their hidden necropolis. They swathed mummified nobles with layer upon layer of wrappings as large as twenty by eighty feet, enough in all to enshroud a house. Some mantles were woven as fine as 250 threads to the inch; others were embroidered with mythological figures requiring as many as two million stitches in twenty shades. The Paracas' obsession to go sumptuously into the hereafter has been justified, in a way. Although most of the mummies at the cores of the big funereal bundles were thrown away in the past, the robes, still rich in color after 2,500 years, are preserved in textile museums throughout the world.

Paracas tombs held little gold compared to the rich booty taken from coastal sites north of Lima that I photographed next from my low-flying plane. Of nearly 2,000 archaeological sites in the Moche valley around Trujillo, Peru, the largest in my lens was a man-made mountain, the Huaca del Sol—Temple of the Sun—built of about 140 million mud bricks. Originally 1,120 feet long, 520 wide, and 150 high, the Huaca del Sol was the largest adobe edifice in the New World.

Empty deserts looked like cratered no-man's-lands of World War I trench warfare; there is little wind in the north to cover excavated tombs with sand. I shot roll after roll of prehistoric roads and pyramids as well as strange patterns of cities and aqueducts barely perceptible on infrared film. Peruvians showed little enthusiasm for my imagined finds. "We already have a hundred times as many ruins as archaeologists to study them. And it's sad to work on devastated tombs."

Until the twentieth century, most of the golden artifacts unearthed by *huaqueros* were melted into shapeless blobs. Even though ceramics were largely disregarded in past centuries, more than a million intact pre-Inca relics have ended up in museums and private collections. The most admired *huacos* of the Mochicas —the people of Moche that prospered between A.D. 100 and 700—are sculpted ceramic water vessels that reveal more details of human and animal behavior than other peoples have ever expressed in a three-dimensional art form. Some depict surgeons and midwives at work; others portray sexual play, little of it procreative.

I used to imagine going back in time to witness a South American kingdom at the summit of its power, and standing on top of a painted adobe pyramid to watch a procession of prelates. But Mochica pottery suggests it might have been rash to drop in unexpectedly; their art betrays obsession with severed heads. Priests slice off lips and noses of captives. A bird pecks the empty eye socket of a naked prisoner bound to a tree; the other eye bulges in terror.

The Mochicas may have been overpowered by the Huari, wiry Andean warriors accustomed to tilling mountainsides so steep that to fall off the farm could be fatal. They, in turn, gave way in the thirteenth century to the Moon Kingdom of Chimor, a dynasty of nine or ten successive kings of the Chimú culture. The kingdom dominated 600 miles of the Pacific coast, ruling from its capital, Chan Chan, in the Moche valley.

To be able to capture the adobe ruins in a single photograph, I had to urge my pilot higher, for Chan Chan still covers five of its original nine square miles. With roughly 50,000 inhabitants, it was the largest pre-Columbian city in South America. At his death, vassals entombed each Chimú king with treasure and hundreds of young women to enhance his enjoyment of the hereafter. His heir built a new richly adorned compound nearby. There are at least nine, possibly as many as ten or eleven, compounds, long since vandalized, at Chan Chan.

The Incas absorbed the Moon Kingdom into their empire in the 1470s. It was a fateful decade. Had oracles of the realm truly been able to see into the future, they would have been dismayed, for those were the years when Christopher Columbus was learning to navigate the high seas and Francisco Pizarro, who would overthrow the Incas, was growing up in Spain.

The Inca generals left undespoiled the Chimú tombs, but banished captured chieftains, goldsmiths, and *huacos* to Cuzco, hub of the Inca universe. Cuzco's polished stone temples housed both Inca and conquered peoples' *huacos* as well as mummies of dead kings. Temple gardens were garnished with golden fountains, and golden hummingbirds sipped droplets of gold from the throats of gilded flowers. Gold would be the undoing of the Incas, for it excited death-defying greed in the Spaniards.

Until 1533, forty years after Europeans happened upon the unexpected continent, the Incas ruled from Cuzco the last great secret empire on earth: Tahuantinsuyu, the Four Quarters of the World. It ranged 2,500 miles along the Andean backbone of South America and the adjacent Pacific coast, from southern Colombia down through Ecuador, Peru, and Bolivia, to central Chile.

"Cuzco was more a compound inhabited by nobles and their retinues than a town as we think of it," according to my friend Dr. Luis A. Pardo. Retired director of the museum and archaeology department of Cuzco's University of San Antonio Abád, Don Luis lived in a house whose front wall was built of stone by the Incas, as with many other houses, hotels, and restaurants in the city center. Since the Inca emperor's artisans worked in stone, many of their spectacular structures have withstood nearly five centuries of earthquake, war, and wrenching urban alteration that began in the sixteenth century with the arrival of the Spaniards. "The city was built in the shape of a puma, evoking the feline cult common to many Andean cultures," said Don Luis. "Avenues cross in slightly trapezoidal

patterns. Doors, windows, and niches also are trapezoids—narrowing at the top —a feature that makes late Inca architecture easily recognizable and helps it survive earthquakes like that of 1950." I had entered the city shortly after nature's sledgehammer blow had hurled stone blocks from Inca buildings onto cobbled streets like big black dice and had torn away walls to reveal second-story bedrooms that looked like theatrical sets.

The Inca highways from north, south, east, and west converge at Cuzco's central square. Few bits of earth have been so saturated with exultation, tragedy, and blood. Idols and mummies of kings were paraded there. At least one hundred pure white llamas a month were sacrificed in routine festivals; fine clothing and food were burned. For deliverance from calamities—pestilence, drought, or reverses in warfare—offerings even included the sacrifice of unblemished children.

An extraordinary fortress, Sacsahuamán, commands a steep rise overlooking Cuzco from the north. Garcilaso de la Vega, the famous chronicler of Inca times and himself half-Inca, wrote that Sacsahuamán was a greater work than the seven wonders of the world—more like pieces of a mountain than mere building stones—and a witness to the majesty of the Incas.

Writers in colonial times, accustomed to thinking of Indians as downtrodden and presumably devoid of creativity, were unwilling to credit the Incas with enough engineering ability to have constructed Sacsahuamán. Surely giants had built it, or the devil, or ancients who used magical herbs for softening and shaping stone. By the twentieth century, authors of drugstore paperbacks were postulating that Sacsahuamán had been built by extraterrestrials. I met a Cuzco doctor who was certain that Martians had constructed the fortress: "Not the little green men, of course. But *big* green men."

The eastern region of the Incas' Four Quarters of the World was the rain-lashed slope of the Andes leading down to the Amazon Basin. The highlanders bartered for bright ceremonial feathers and recruited bowmen there, but they never conquered the forest tribes, who would not come out in the open to fight. One week's march below Cuzco the Incas built a magnificent citadel of stone on an almost unseen and inaccessible ridge. The Spanish conquerors never found the outpost. A deserted, jungle-grown fragment of the empire, it remained an untouched time capsule until its discovery in 1911.

It was on muleback that I first climbed the cliff to Machu Picchu's temples and terraces in 1948. Six years later I stayed at the then tiny hostel during several days of filming, and the only tourists who stopped by were two Austrian climbers. Now several jets a day fly tourists of many nationalities to Cuzco. More than 1 million passengers have ridden the train down into the Urubamba gorge to discover the lost city of the Incas for themselves. Hundreds of hardier souls have even hiked the remnants of an Inca road all the exhausting way to Machu Picchu from Cuzco or from a train stop partway there, at Kilometer 88.

To bind the realm together, royal highways crossed mountains and deserts, and suspension bridges spanned foaming rivers. In Inca times and for centuries thereafter the greatest bridge of all soared high over the Río Apurimac, the tributary that I traced to the ultimate Amazon source in 1971. As the mile-deep Apurimac gorge cuts Cuzco off from the western reaches of the Andes and the coast, the bridge was a key to imperial conquest. It was built and constantly renewed by craftsmen of Carahuasi, a town perched on the rim of the gorge. They

spun fibers drawn from the great leaves of the *cabuya,* a century plant, into cables thicker than a man's thigh. Hundreds of peasants hauling in unison stretched the cables across the void to create a suspension bridge. To reach the span, travelers had to switchback down a cliff-hanging trail.

"The gorge narrowed . . . apparently preventing all exit from the sunless and threatening ravine," wrote American archaeologist E. George Squier in the 1860s. He sighted the bridge "swinging high in a graceful curve, between the precipices on either side, looking wonderfully frail and gossamer-like." Yet the great Apurimac bridge had been a conduit for mighty armies.

In November 1533, when the Spanish invaders set out along the royal road to Cuzco after garroting the Inca Atahuallpa, Pizarro sent Hernando De Soto and seventy cavalrymen ahead to capture the Apurimac bridge. Alerted, the keepers of the bridge burned it. But Spanish luck held; the summer rains were late. De Soto's cavalry swam the usually impassable Apurimac without loss. Though enormously outnumbered, the Spaniards fought on to seize the capital of the Inca Empire and its golden gardens.

I first saw a film replica of the Apurimac bridge in a 1929 movie starring Ramón Navarro and Lily Damita: *The Bridge of San Luis Rey.* Later I discovered the 1927 novel on which the film was based. It gripped me from the very first sentence: "On Friday noon, July the twentieth, 1714, the finest bridge in all Peru broke and precipitated five travelers into the gulf below."

The story of "Why did this happen to those five?" precipitated its author, New Jersey schoolteacher Thornton Wilder, into the mainstream of world literature. The characters in *The Bridge*—an allegory about the invincibility of the human spirit—spoke to me so eloquently that I became sure I would travel someday to Peru and even to the site of the span.

And I did. In 1973, while preparing an article—as well as my book, *The Incredible Incas*—for the National Geographic Society, I learned that one hundred years ago a masonry arch was built across the river and the great suspension bridge was left to rot. It collapsed about 1895. I set out to look for the site.

When I descended into the suddenly hot and heavy air at the bottom of the gorge, beset with sharp cacti and blood-sucking sand flies, I found that landslides had destroyed the approaches. I decided then to search for one of the lesser Apurimac bridges described in yellowing pages of histories about civil wars among the conquistadores—even though leading historians and archaeologists insisted that no such span remained.

I chartered a plane and flew up the narrow gorge of the Apurimac from jungle to source, photographing suspension bridges from the air. Back on the ground I traveled to several sites only to discover after arduous descents that steel cables had replaced fiber ropes, which villagers had kept renewing long after Inca times. Finally I got wind of an abandoned *keshwa chaca,* a grass-rope bridge, far up the Apurimac in Canas Province some 11,000 feet above sea level. I made one last trek and found it still hanging sixty feet above the river, gleaming like Inca gold in the afternoon sun.

As I clawed down a cliff to reach it, a voice cautioned, "Don't cross! The bridge is dying!" An Indian appeared. Luis Choqueneira, who wore clusters of wildflowers in his hat, as most of the Canas peasants do, said he was one of the *chaca camayocs,* keepers of the bridge. I explained my long quest, and he said, "We

are going to rebuild the bridge, as we have done ever since the Incas ordered it. Come back next year if you want to watch."

When the time came, Sue and I stayed at Luis's home, storing there the gifts of bread and *chicha*—Indian corn beer—that would ensure cooperation for picture taking. Throughout the community of thatched houses scattered about the high country, children pounded sheaves of *coyo,* a tough bunch grass that grows abundantly in the vicinity, to make it supple. Women spun and braided it into finger-size cordage.

Hundreds of Indians toted to the bridge site about 22,000 feet of grass rope. Men twisted and braided it into six massive cables. The following day they floated messenger lines made of grass from bank to bank, pulled the cables across the gorge, anchored the bridge, and caged the sides so that not even a child could fall through.

On the final day everyone came to celebrate. Men, women, and children wore fresh wildflowers in their hats. Three old *chaca camayocs* wove a footing of twigs to finish their work. In fourteen working hours they had completely rebuilt the one-hundred-foot span. All the while, a ritual fire of coca leaves and sequin-spangled corn smoldered by the bridge foundations.

Luis let Sue and me be the first to cross. We ventured out over the torrent swollen with summer rain, a little giddy with the swaying of the bridge and with the ritual smoke that wreathed the faces of the tough and wonderful men of Canas. They cheered us on, toasting with flagons of *chicha* to the health of the *keshwa chaca.*

Some Indians tossed their hats into the air. The blossoms whirled away like careless butterflies snatched by a downdraft and disappeared into the void beneath the last Inca bridge.

The adobe bell tower, *above,* has withstood violent storms and earthquakes for more than two centuries. It was built beside a massive colonial church at Sabaya, on the Bolivian altiplano, when the Spanish empire ruled this land. The three crosses of calvary are of straw. *Left,* a thousand years earlier, pre-Inca peoples built soaring adobe burial tombs, called *chullpas,* for their chieftains. *Chullpas* at hundreds of sites throughout the altiplano have been profaned long since by thieves who entered the doors that all face east.

o v e r l e a f
His poncho held like an apron, Pablito Quispe offers me *rocoto* (hot red chili peppers) after herding his llamas into the lofty village of Queros, Peru. Queros trails are so steep that even sure-footed pack llamas bringing corn from a valley farm have fallen from the cliff.

After Inca rule crumbled, many Indians fled to their ancestral mountains. Andrés Apasa, *right,* dwells in Queros, Peru, a stone village high on the Amazon side of the Andes. He speaks Quechua, the Inca tongue. Alongside the trail to Queros, *opposite*—too high for growing corn—women tend potatoes, the Andean peoples' greatest gift to humankind. In the highlands of Ecuador, *below right,* northern bastion of the Inca Empire, Old World cereals are cultivated—but none have the religious and mystic power of native corn, a sacred crop.

o v e r l e a f
Llamas circle a water hole two and one half miles above sea level on the Bolivian altiplano. The Incas skirted this desolate land, thinly peopled then as now by Aymara-speaking natives who are the owners of these pack animals. There are no wild llamas; all live in symbiotic relationship with humans of the highlands.

Above, women herd llamas homeward, past the ruined fortress of Sacsahuamán (many-colored falcon) guarding the heights above Cuzco, Peru. Its ramparts survive: fitted stones weighing up to 350 tons were too massive for Spaniards to carry into Cuzco for building churches. *Opposite above,* a hamlet's thatched roofs, adobe walls, and stone stairways in central Ecuador appear to be almost unchanged since Inca times. *Opposite,* as agriculture gave birth to Andean civilizations, sowing, watering, and harvesting became intensely ceremonial. Even today highland Indians revere Pacha Mama, the earth mother.

o v e r l e a f
Machu Picchu, lost citadel of the Incas, clings to a crag in the cloud forest of Peru. Though archaeologists began to investigate the ruins in 1911, the circumstances of Machu Picchu's existence and abandonment are still uncertain.

In Inca times, pure white llamas like the newborn, *far left,* were thought to be more *huaca*—holy—than others, and were singled out for religious rituals when grown. In 1972, I watched natives of Lake Titicaca's Island of the Sun sacrifice a white llama to the earth mother to insure her fecundity. Sorcerers slit its jugular vein, drink its blood, scatter some on fields, and bury its head and hooves, *left.* The llama arrives festooned with serpentine and loaded with a green charm bundle of bread, flowers, popcorn, cigarettes, and coca leaves, *opposite.* The victim is honored during the long day's alcoholic festivity and its demise at sundown is orchestrated prayerfully.

o v e r l e a f
The Incas prepared *chuño*— dehydrated potatoes—by scattering them in midwinter to freeze by night and thaw in the morning sun. Their Andean descendants still do so, gathering them into piles and trampling the softened potatoes with their bare feet to press out the moisture. Spread again until dried, *chuño* keeps for years.

In a land where climate varies from tropical to polar in four vertical miles, corn thrives from sea level to the 12,500-foot Pampa de Anta near Cuzco, Peru, where Bernadina Orccosupa, *above left,* spreads the cobs to dry in the sunny but freezing month of June, winter in the southern Andes. Hilarión Quispe, *above,* lives in Queros, a hidden enclave of Inca tradition high on the Amazon side of the mountains and a week's walk from Cuzco. His potato farm perches on slopes above the village and his cornfields cling to tropical hillsides far below. Men and women carry corn from a store-room to dry on a patio, *left.*

o v e r l e a f
The last of the lost empires, Spain's and Portugal's, endured three centuries, until the 1820s. The Spaniards laid out their colonial towns in grids. Coipasa, *left,* still remains unchanged at the edge of a great brine lake on the Bolivian altiplano: a central square with its dominant church, city hall, and garrison, framed by lesser rectangles of urban streets. When the Indians lived too far away to attend, the church went to them, as with this solitary chapel in the Bolivian Andes, *right.* Its steeple stands apart, the better to resist earthquakes.

Two miles above sea level in the Andes of Peru, the last of the Inca suspension bridges—which once served as conduits of an empire—spans the Apurimac, the source river of the Amazon. On 6 January, Epiphany, a religious feast day, when the river is swelling with summer rains and there is neither planting nor harvesting to be done, the peasants of Canas Province begin to renew the bridge—an annual ceremony. Women spin tough bunch grass into rope, *opposite.* Men braid the rope into six stout cables, haul them across the gorge, and a specialist cages the sides, *right.* On the third day, amid great rejoicing, women cross the new bridge for the first time, *below right.* I felt as happy as they to have discovered, in 1973, a living reminder of Inca splendors.

Seen from 21,500 feet above sea
level at the Chilean border, the
world's densest concentration of
lofty volcanoes studs the southwest
corner of Bolivia, *above.* Italians
who in 1939 climbed to the crater of
Licancabur, *foreground,* discovered
remains of Inca shrines, idols of
silver and shell, and firewood.
At remote Micaypata, in southern
Peru, I pose for a portrait with
village men who put on their
Sunday ponchos for the occasion,
opposite above.
o v e r l e a f
Portugal still ruled half of South
America when Ouro Prêto (Black
Gold) was built by wealthy Brazilian
miners in the mountains north of
Rio de Janeiro. Its poets and
intellectuals, excited by the
American revolution, conspired in
vain against the Europeans. After
independence, mines failed
and hard times precluded
modernization of Ouro Prêto,
relic of a golden age of empire.

Every year I migrate south for a few months with a notebook and camera. In 1989 I traveled to Ecuador's Galapagos Islands, Peru's guano islands, Chile's Easter Island, and on to Argentina and Brazil.

In Brazil, I joined Amazon river pilot Guilherme Robelo on the bridge of the TSS *Stella Solaris* while he brought the cruise ship to anchor near Belém, recalling my wide-eyed first arrival in town fifty-four years earlier—decked out in coat and tie. Guilherme said, "Today I wouldn't know where to shop for a necktie in Brazil."

We hit the beach in sports attire to buy a crocodile-tooth necklace for the ship's first mate. Except for fewer caged animals, the waterfront market, Ver-O-Peso, still looks and smells the same. Yet from the air—missionary Don Egan took me up in an ultralight—it appeared that Belém, with its million inhabitants, had become a cluster of skyscrapers set in emerald: from the far shores of the rivers Pará and Guamá, which half-surround the city, unbroken rain forest extends to the horizon.

A ribbon of pavement runs out Belém's back door 1,300 miles to Brasília, the glistening capital built on the central plateau nearly three decades ago to accelerate westward expansion. Since then Brazil's population has more than doubled, quintupling in my lifetime.

The unrestrained birthrate and the unflagging urge to erect new cities on pristine plains have driven landless families and developers 1,700 miles inland to Rondônia, the new state halfway across the continent on the Bolivian frontier. In 1960 only seven trucks made it to Pôrto Velho, Rondônia's capital; by 1984 the highway was paved. But there is no pristine plain in Rondônia; even by 1988, rain forests still covered three-quarters of its territory. In order to tame the wilderness, the pioneers cut trees with chain saws as if they were enormous weeds that spoiled a vision of black asphalt roads flanked by yellow corn or herds of white cebu cattle. They name their new acres, still cluttered with felled trees and tangled branches, Nova Aurora, Nova Esperança, Novo Horizonte (New Dawn, New Hope, New Horizon). . . .

In August, the last month of the dry season, colonists put the torch to the felled forests. Drafts suck dry brush into the incandescent vortices of fire storms, and flames soar higher than the towering crowns of the Brazil nut trees—which, by law, must be left standing. The charred residue of intricate ecosystems swirls up and out of sight. Smoke reddens the noonday sun, and in the gloom cattle head prematurely homeward. The ashes of August fall into the canopy of the rain forest and mingle with the dust of newly cut clearings, adding fertility to the soil and besmudging laundry hung to dry by settlers who live along red earthen roads that penetrate the jungle. In September rains begin to wash the ash into Amazon headwaters. November thunderstorms whip ankle-deep dust into axle-deep quagmires. By year's end the only road in Rondônia still easily traveled is BR–364, the paved trans-Brazil highway that bisects the state.

In January 1988 there was a rumor of a "tin rush"—40,000 men trekking into a Rondônia forest to pan for alluvial tin. I borrowed a van from a Brazilian friend, Amaral Gurgel, who manufactures cars and names them after himself. I drove the Gurgel down BR–364 to see the strike. At a fueling station a dozen heavyset drivers of eighteen-wheel trailer trucks joked about their big bellies, their "*calos sexualis*." A sign announced surgical costs at Hospital São Lucas in Ji-Paraná City: CONSULTATION $1, APPENDECTOMY $60, HYSTERECTOMY $150, CESAREAN $80, NORMAL DELIVERY $40, ABORTION $40.

Heading west on a penetration road, Linha C–75, I came to a slough churned by heavy rain and overloaded trucks. I parked the Gurgel beside the last farmhouse and floundered on foot through the forest, alongside a road resembling a viscous river strewn with bemired vehicles. I became part of a column of *garimpeiros* (prospectors), who shouldered awkward loads originally intended to be trucked: canned food, kerosene, hoses, hammocks, axes, and shovels. Foot traffic was so continuous that waiting vultures could not safely get at the bloated body of a half-naked youth lying, ignored, beside the path. His throat had been slit.

Eventually the mud widened into a road through a shantytown of shelters and shops built of black plastic sheets draped over wooden poles. Entrepreneurs of the newborn settlement, Marilandia, offered groceries, mining equipment, gasoline, liquor, pharmaceuticals, and liaisons with prostitutes as young as thirteen—all at prices five times costlier than in the nearest town. Beyond Marilandia, the road led to a bewildering patchwork of pits dug into the floor of the uncut forest. Wildcat miners sloshed waist-deep in muddy water, panning for nuggets of tin ore the size of corn kernels. The prospector who discovered the ore named the strike Garimpo Bom Futuro; most of the miners now called it Garimpo Filho de Puta. In the murky light of afternoon rain, trees blocked my view; I saw only a few hundred of the alleged 40,000 "tin rush" wildcatters.

No governmental presence had existed in the region when tin was discovered on Indian land, and I found none when I got there sixty days later. "Gunfire starts at sundown and goes on all night," a pharmacist told me. "Why? Because you can earn more with a gun. Today I certified sixteen deaths."

I had no wish to remain and be certified. But hitchhiking out of the Bom Futuro slough on a stormy night became awkward. My flashlight batteries failed, I tripped over branches covered with ants and wasps, and as in a terrifying nightmare, I nearly got run over by the side-slipping rear wheels of a truck—its tire chains thrashing like cement-mixers—when my feet got stuck in the mud.

Later, riding in the bed of a truck in the dark and slashing rain, I spotted my Gurgel beside the first farmhouse we came to, and pounded on the roof of the cab until the driver stopped and let me off.

I knocked. The farmhouse owner was slow to open the door to a bedraggled stranger. I introduced myself to Sebastião and Leni Martins and six sleepy-eyed children who crowded the doorway. Their father said, "Glad you're not a *garimpeiro*. We work the land; they ruin it." Pretty blond Cleonice drew me a pail of wellwater for bathing, Leni cooked a meal, and Sebastião ordered Valdir, the eldest son, to give up his bed to me. Sometime before dawn, when I unlatched the door to go out and relieve myself, several wet dogs and a rooster burst in out of the rain and jumped onto the beds. Leni drove them outside with a broom and lusty curses.

In the morning Sebastião showed me his farm, New Canaan. "Two years ago I bought 140 hectares of worthless jungle for $2,000." Now plantations of corn and rice ripened in fields of charred logs that point every which way. Beyond his farm lie Indian lands.

By October 1992 the tribesmen still hiding in the Rondônia rain forest and their forebears will have held out exactly 500 years since the "Admiral of the Ocean Sea" laid claim to a New World beach in the name of a European king. But my Urueu-Wau-Wau friends do not realize that they are among the last Native Americans in the hemisphere to succumb to civilization. The only aspect of New World conquest that concerns them is how to get rid of interlopers who are laying charred rectangles on the natural curves of their land. In any case, Rondônia's forest Indians do not keep time by clock and calendar and are not likely to join any quincentennial festivities.

Or so it seemed to me, as, with very mixed feelings, I helped Sebastião Martins's brother-in-law nail a crudely lettered sign—SITIO NOVO MUNDO (New World Ranch)—to the only tree left standing on his homestead.

overleaf
Even before the ashes cool, homesteads rise from the fallen forest of Rondônia, Brazil, *left*. Amid the ruins of an old ecosystem, Italina Panum and her fiancé, Elvino Kuak, look ahead to a new life, *right*.

pages 202–203
"They are rather like birds or wild animals," wrote the first European chronicler ever to see the forest Indians of South America, in April of 1500. "Their bodies are so clean and so beautiful." Nearly five centuries later I came upon a few of their descendants bathing in one of the infinite sources of the Amazon.

INDEX

o v e r l e a f
Roulim de Moura, a Brazilian lumber town, did not exist in 1980, when lush forests covered most of Rondônia.

o v e r l e a f
Roulim de Moura, a Brazilian lumber town, did not exist in 1980, when lush forests covered most of Rondônia.